HR Toolbox for Start-Ups

Meenakshi

notionpress.com

INDIA • SINGAPORE • MALAYSIA

ISBN

Hardcase 979-8-89556-618-3
Paperback 979-8-89544-279-1

DEDICATION

Vidushi, my daughter

CONTENTS

Preface 11

Chapter 1: HR Architecture 21

Chapter 2: Organization Structure 32

Chapter 3: Organizational Culture 53

Chapter 4: Strategic HR 60

    How do we future-proof? 76

    The case of Industry 4.0 80

Chapter 5: Role of HRBP 85

    Envision 90

        HR Strategy 90

        Organizational Structure 93

        Organizational Culture 96

    Workforce Planning 100

        Job Design 103

    Hire 107

        Recruitment Policy 107

        Recruitment Procedures 111

        Job Descriptions 114

        Onboarding 118

Manage 122

    Performance Management 122

    Compensations Management 127

    Employee Relations... 131

Inspire 135

    Learning & Development 135

    Engagement... 140

    Recognition 144

Care 149

    Health, Safety, and Security 149

    Stress at work and staff wellbeing 153

Exit 156

How to monitor the HRBP team's Performance...................... 160

    Employee engagement.. 164

    Knowledge accessibility 168

    Workforce optimization.. 173

    Learning capacity 178

Chapter 6: Talent Acquisition.. 183

Behavioral interviewing 186

    What to look for in candidates?.............................. 186

    How to write interview questions? 187

    How to create rating scales? 188

Online Recruiting 188

    Company website... 188

    Internet ad campaigns 189

    Social media 189

    Online job sites... 190

    Implement pre-screening tools and skills assessments.... 190

    Dedicated contact sourcing 191

Online recruitment software 191

Video advertising 192

Video interviews 192

Onboarding leaders 193

Chapter 7: Talent Management **196**

Developing a talent pool 200

Succession Planning 200

Capacity Building 203

Relationship building 203

Bursary program 203

Internship Program 204

Apprentice program 204

Connecting Talent to Value 204

Chapter 8: Compensation Management **206**

Principles of compensation 210

Components of Compensation 211

Direct Compensation 211

Indirect Compensation 211

Basic wages 211

Dearness allowance 212

Incentives 212

Bonus 212

Non-monetary benefits 212

Commissions 213

Fringe benefits 213

Profit sharing 213

Factors in deciding the compensation 214

External factors 214

Internal factors 214

Wage and salary surveys 214

Wage Curve 215

Variable pay 216

Types of Variable Pay Plans 216

    Individual 216

    Group/Team 216

    Organization-wide 217

International compensation management 217

    Base salary 217

    Benefits 217

    Allowance 217

    Incentives 218

    Long-term benefits 218

A closer look at total rewards 219

Chapter 9: HR Technology 220

HR Technology to Work Technology 224

    HR Technology 224

    Work Technology 225

Evolution of HR Functions to Work Technology 226

HR Tech Architecture 226

Four stages of HR Tech Market 227

AI is now here 228

Experience economy 229

    Candidate experience 229

    Onboarding experience 229

    Team engagement 229

    Tools and Access 229

    Learning & Development 229

Performance...229

Leaves 229

Rewards & Recognition 230

Travel 230

Roles & KRA 230

Exit 230

Rethinking ground-up 230

Common HR pain-points...230

Digital employee themes and strategies 231

Digital HR Core 232

Flexible & Global HR Core...232

Digital recruiting, hiring, and onboarding................233

Digital Social Collaboration 234

Mobilize HR 235

Move to cloud...236

Chapter 10: HR Analytics..**237**

Strategic management 237

Workforce Planning and Staffing.................................239

Talent Management...241

Total Rewards 242

Risk Management 242

Financial Management..242

Succession planning...243

Employee Engagement 244

Chapter 11: Employee Engagement **245**

Determinants of employee engagement 247

Work environment 247

Leadership..249

Team and co-worker relationship................................. 251

Training and career development.............................. 252

Compensation.. 254

Organizational policies.. 256

References *261*

PREFACE

Welcome to "HR Toolbox for Start-Ups."

This book is crafted specifically for those who are pioneering new ventures and need to establish a robust HR foundation. As many of you are aware, starting a new business is a thrilling endeavor filled with opportunities and challenges. One of the most critical aspects of ensuring long-term success lies in creating an effective Human Resources function that supports growth; fosters a positive culture and drives performance. This book is designed to be your 'strategic guide' through this intricate journey, providing you with the knowledge and tools necessary to build and sustain an effective HR function from scratch.

Our journey begins with the foundational concept of HR Architecture. In this chapter, we delve into how to lay the groundwork for building a successful HR function. Understanding HR Architecture involves more than just organizing processes; it is about developing, acquiring, contracting, and forming strategic alliances with human capital. This chapter provides a comprehensive framework for designing an HR system that aligns with your start-up's unique needs and strategic goals. By focusing on these core elements, you will be well-equipped to create an HR framework that supports your organization's vision and mission.

Once the architectural foundation is in place, we turn our attention to the organizational structure. The second chapter explores how to align your organizational structure with your overarching strategy. This involves examining various organizational structures, including vertical, matrix, and open boundary models, and understanding how these structures impact your operations and growth. We discuss the importance of designing an organizational structure that is not only functional but also adaptable to the changing needs of your start-up. This section will guide you in creating a structure that supports scalability and efficiency as your organization evolves.

Organizational culture is another crucial aspect of your start-up's success. In the third chapter, we dive into the types of organizational cultures and their effects on employee behaviors and performance. Culture is often described as the heartbeat of an organization, influencing everything from employee engagement to overall job satisfaction. This chapter provides insights into building and nurturing a positive organizational culture that aligns with your start-up's values and goals. Understanding and shaping your organizational culture will help you create a work environment that attracts and retains top talent while fostering a sense of belonging and purpose among employees.

Strategic HR is about ensuring that your HR practices are aligned with your business objectives. The fourth chapter explores the benefits of strategic planning and how to develop a strategic HR plan that supports your start-up's long-term goals. This includes setting clear HR objectives, adapting to industry changes, and preparing for future challenges. Strategic HR planning is essential for positioning your HR function as a key driver of business success, and this chapter offers practical guidance on how to achieve that alignment.

As your start-up grows, the role of HR Business Partners (HRBPs) becomes increasingly important. The fifth chapter outlines the various responsibilities of HRBPs, from envisioning and hiring to managing, inspiring, and caring for employees. Effective HRBPs are instrumental in aligning HR practices with business strategy and ensuring that HR initiatives support organizational goals. This chapter also provides guidance on monitoring HRBP performance to ensure that they are meeting their objectives and contributing to the overall success of the organization.

Talent acquisition is a critical component of building a strong HR function. The sixth chapter focuses on best practices for attracting and hiring the right talent. This includes behavioral interviewing techniques, online recruiting strategies, and effective onboarding processes. Talent acquisition is not just about filling positions; it's about finding individuals who will contribute to your start-up's success and align with its values. This chapter provides practical tools and strategies for creating a recruitment process that identifies and attracts top talent.

Once you have acquired talent, managing that talent effectively becomes paramount. The seventh chapter explores strategies for talent management, including developing a talent pool, building relationships, and implementing programs such as bursaries, internships, and apprenticeships. Connecting talent to value is essential for ensuring ongoing engagement and development. This chapter offers insights into creating a talent management system that supports employee growth and contributes to the overall success of your start-up.

Compensation management is another key area of focus. The eighth chapter discusses the principles of compensation, including the components of compensation packages, factors influencing pay decisions, and international compensation management. A well-structured compensation system is vital for attracting and retaining talent, and this chapter provides guidance on designing a rewards system that aligns with your start-up's goals and values.

In the ninth chapter, we explore the role of technology in HR. Technology has transformed HR practices, and understanding its impact is crucial for modern HR management. This chapter examines the evolution of HR technology into Work Technology, including digital recruiting, onboarding, and social collaboration. It also discusses how to leverage technology to enhance HR efficiency and employee experience, providing insights into building a technology-driven HR function that supports your start-up's needs.

HR analytics is the focus of the tenth chapter. Data-driven decision-making is essential for effective HR management, and this chapter provides an overview of HR analytics, including its applications in strategic management, workforce planning, talent management, and more. By using analytics to inform decisions and track performance, you can drive organizational success and make informed HR decisions.

Finally, the eleventh chapter addresses employee engagement, which is crucial for achieving high performance and job satisfaction. This chapter explores the determinants of employee engagement and offers strategies for creating an environment where employees are motivated, committed, and aligned with the organization's goals. Engaging employees is essential for fostering a positive work culture and driving overall success.

This book is designed for HR professionals, managers, and leaders in start-ups who are looking to build a strong HR function from scratch. Whether you are a founder setting up your first HR systems or an HR manager tasked with scaling a growing start-up, this book provides practical insights and actionable strategies to help you navigate the complexities of HR management.

As you embark on this journey, we hope that this book serves as a valuable resource in creating a thriving and resilient organization. Building a strong HR function is not just about managing employees; it's about creating a foundation for success and ensuring that your start-up can achieve its long-term goals. Thank you for joining us on this journey, and may this book guide you in achieving excellence in HR and building a strong foundation for your start-up's future success.

Foundation for HR Excellence: The book provides a comprehensive foundation for building an effective HR function from scratch. It covers essential topics such as HR Architecture, Organizational Structure, and Strategic HR, offering practical insights for creating a robust HR framework in a start-up environment.

Tailored for Start-Ups: Unlike generic HR books, this guide is specifically designed for start-ups. It addresses the unique challenges and opportunities faced by new ventures, making it highly relevant for HR Business Partners working in fast-paced, evolving start-up environments.

Strategic HR Planning: The book offers detailed strategies for aligning HR practices with business objectives. It covers how to develop a strategic HR plan, set objectives, and adapt to industry changes, ensuring that HR initiatives support the overall goals of the start-up.

Innovative Talent Acquisition Techniques: With a focus on behavioral interviewing, online recruiting, and effective onboarding, the book provides cutting-edge methods for attracting and retaining top talent. This is crucial for start-ups aiming to build a high-performing team.

Comprehensive Talent Management: The guide explores various talent management strategies, including developing talent pools, building relationships, and implementing programs like internships and apprenticeships. It provides actionable insights for managing and nurturing talent effectively.

Effective Compensation Management: Understanding compensation is critical for start-ups to attract and retain talent. The book delves into compensation principles, components, and international management, offering valuable guidance on designing a competitive rewards system.

Leveraging HR Technology: As technology transforms HR practices, the book examines how to utilize HR and Work Technology effectively. It covers digital recruiting, onboarding, and collaboration tools, helping HR Business Partners stay ahead in the tech-driven landscape.

Data-Driven HR with Analytics: The book emphasizes the importance of HR analytics for making informed decisions. It provides insights into using data for strategic management, workforce planning, and employee engagement, helping HR Business Partners drive performance through analytics.

Building a Positive Organizational Culture: A positive culture is crucial for start-up success. The book discusses how to build and sustain an organizational culture that aligns with the start-up's values and goals, enhancing employee satisfaction and engagement.

Holistic Approach to Employee Engagement: Employee engagement is vital for productivity and retention. The book offers strategies for fostering engagement, ensuring that employees are motivated, committed, and aligned with the start-up's mission and values.

This book is an invaluable resource for HR Business Partners in start-ups, offering practical, tailored guidance on building a strong HR function, managing talent, and leveraging technology to drive organizational success.

"HR Toolbox for Start-Ups" is particularly invaluable for start-ups in the IT industry

...due to its tailored approach to the unique demands and rapid changes characteristic of technology-focused ventures. In the fast-paced world of IT, where innovation and agility are crucial, this book offers targeted insights and practical strategies to address the specific challenges faced by tech start-ups.

Firstly, the book provides a robust framework for establishing an HR function from scratch. For IT start-ups, this is especially important as they often operate with limited resources and need to prioritize efficiency. The comprehensive sections on HR Architecture and Organizational Structure help these companies set up foundational HR systems that are scalable and adaptable to their evolving needs. This ensures that HR practices align with the dynamic nature of the IT sector, where project demands and team compositions can shift rapidly.

The book's focus on Strategic HR is particularly relevant for IT start-ups, which must continuously align their human capital strategies with fast-changing technological trends and market conditions. By offering strategies for developing a strategic HR plan, setting objectives, and planning for future growth, the book equips IT leaders with the tools needed to stay ahead of the curve and maintain a competitive edge.

Talent acquisition and management are critical for IT start-ups, where attracting and retaining skilled professionals is a significant challenge. The book delves into advanced techniques such as behavioral interviewing and online recruiting, tailored to the IT industry's requirements. These methods help start-ups identify candidates with the technical skills and cultural fit necessary for success in a high-stakes environment. Additionally, the section on Talent Management provides guidance on building and nurturing talent pools, implementing internship and apprenticeship programs, and developing career growth pathways, all of which are crucial for maintaining a skilled and motivated workforce in the tech industry.

Compensation management is another area where the book provides substantial value. In the IT industry, competitive compensation packages are essential to attract top talent. The book offers detailed insights into designing compensation structures, including principles of compensation, variable pay plans, and international considerations. This information helps start-ups craft attractive and equitable reward systems that can compete with larger tech firms and retain high-performing employees.

As IT start-ups increasingly rely on technology to drive HR functions, the book's focus on HR Technology is crucial. It explores the transition from traditional HR technology to Work Technology, covering digital recruiting, onboarding, and collaboration tools. These insights are invaluable for tech start-ups that must leverage cutting-edge tools to enhance HR efficiency and employee experience in a technology-driven workspace.

Furthermore, the book emphasizes the importance of HR Analytics, providing a framework for using data to drive strategic decisions. For IT start-ups, where data is integral to business operations, applying data-driven insights to HR practices helps optimize workforce planning, manage performance, and enhance employee engagement.

Finally, the book addresses the importance of building a positive organizational culture and fostering employee engagement. For IT start-ups, where team cohesion and motivation directly impact innovation and productivity, creating a supportive and engaging work environment is vital. The book provides strategies for developing a culture that aligns with the start-up's values and goals, ensuring that employees remain committed and enthusiastic about their work.

In summary, this book is a crucial resource for IT start-ups, offering specialized guidance on building and managing an effective HR function in a rapidly evolving industry. Its practical advice on strategic HR planning, talent management, compensation, technology, and culture is designed to help tech start-ups thrive and achieve long-term success.

Meenakshi

| Author | Workforce Management Consultant | IIM Shillong |

CHAPTER 1

HR ARCHITECTURE

The Question

As an HR team, the foundational question we need to address is how to effectively build our human resources. This question encompasses several key considerations: Where do we begin? What approach should guide our decisions? Should we focus on hiring skilled and experienced professionals, or should we recruit interns and provide them with training? Is it more advantageous to develop capabilities within the organization, or would it be better to outsource certain functions to external companies?

To navigate these questions, we turn to a concept known as HR Architecture. This framework helps us identify the specific skills required and assess their value within the organization. It essentially serves as a blueprint for structuring our human resources in alignment with our strategic goals.

Understanding HR Architecture involves analyzing four key quadrants that illustrate different aspects of skill management and organizational development. Each quadrant provides insights into various approaches to building and enhancing human resources.

Hiring Skilled and Experienced Professionals: This approach focuses on bringing in individuals who already possess the specific skills and expertise needed. By hiring professionals with proven track records, we can quickly address immediate skill gaps and benefit from their existing knowledge and capabilities. This strategy is often used when specialized skills are critical for the organization's success and when there is a need for rapid deployment of expertise.

Recruiting and Training Interns: Alternatively, organizations may choose to hire interns or entry-level candidates and invest in their development through training programs. This approach can be advantageous for cultivating long-term talent and building a pipeline of skilled employees who are aligned with the company's culture and values. Investing in training can also be a cost-effective strategy, as it allows the organization to shape the skills and knowledge of its workforce according to its specific needs.

Building Internal Capabilities: Developing capabilities within the organization involves upskilling existing employees and fostering internal growth. This approach focuses on leveraging and expanding the potential of the current workforce. By providing opportunities for professional development and career advancement, the organization can enhance its internal talent pool and improve employee retention. This strategy is often used to create a more resilient and adaptable workforce that can meet future challenges.

Subcontracting to External Companies: Outsourcing certain functions to external providers can be a viable option when specialized skills are needed on a temporary basis or when it is more cost-effective than developing those skills in-house. Subcontracting allows the organization to access external expertise and resources without the long-term commitment of hiring full-time employees. This approach can be particularly useful for non-core activities or for projects requiring specialized knowledge that is not available internally.

By examining these four quadrants, we can better understand our options for building and managing human resources. Each approach has its own advantages and considerations, and the choice depends on the organization's specific needs, goals, and resources. As we embark on our HR journey, this framework will guide us in making informed decisions about how to structure and develop our human resources to support organizational success.

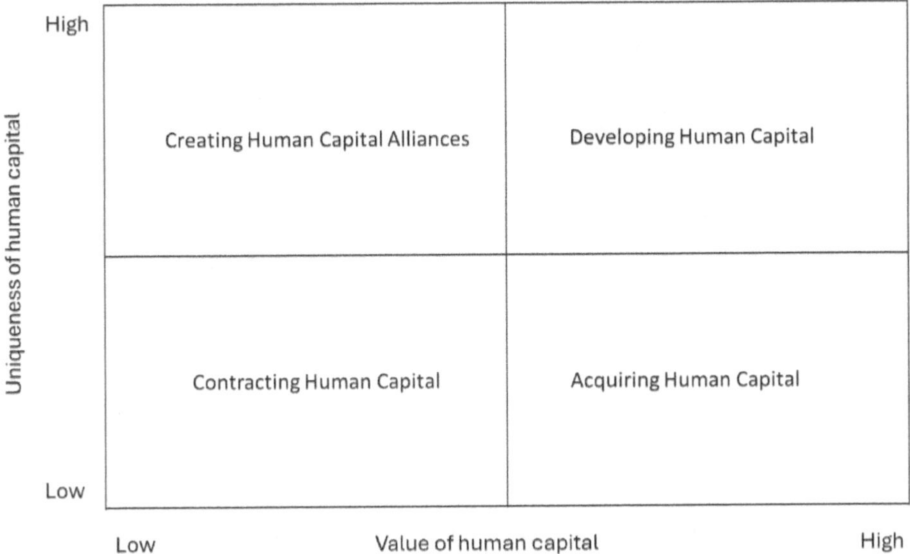

Figure 1: HR Architecture

Developing Human Capital

Human Capital is both valuable and unique. Organizations are more likely to employ people internally when their skills are organization specific. Organization-specific skills are not available in the labor market.

With few alternative sources for unique skills, firms are more likely to develop them internally. In addition to uniqueness, skills within this quadrant are valuable. Their strategic benefit exceeds the managerial and bureaucratic costs associated with their development and deployment.

Internally developing human capital helps firms realize the benefits of these employees in terms of their value-creating potential. Because employees in this skill group possess abilities that are both valuable and unique, we can view them as core employees, who may serve as a source of competitive advantage.

Human capital represents a crucial and distinctive asset for organizations, playing a pivotal role in their overall success and competitive edge. This form of capital encompasses the skills, knowledge, and abilities of employees that are integral to the organization's operations and strategic goals. When it comes to human capital, those skills that are highly specialized and tailored to the specific needs of an organization become particularly significant. These organization-specific skills are not typically available in the broader labor market, making them especially valuable.

The rarity of these specialized skills means that firms often invest in developing them internally rather than seeking external candidates. When a skill set is unique to an organization, it is often because these skills have been cultivated through specific training, experience, or institutional knowledge that cannot easily be replicated elsewhere. This internal development is not just about filling a gap; it's about fostering a competitive advantage. The organization invests time, resources, and effort to nurture these skills, believing that the benefits derived from such investments will outweigh the managerial and bureaucratic costs involved in their cultivation and utilization.

The strategic value of these unique skills is substantial. Employees who possess them contribute significantly to the organization's success by enabling it to perform tasks and address challenges that are beyond the reach of competitors. The investment in developing such specialized human capital reflects a long-term vision, aiming to harness the full potential of these employees to create value that translates into a competitive edge. The strategic benefits include enhanced efficiency, innovation, and adaptability, which are essential for maintaining and strengthening the organization's market position.

Moreover, the development of organization-specific skills often leads to the creation of a core group of employees who are central to the organization's strategy and operations. These core employees are distinguished not only by their specialized skills but also by their deep understanding of the organization's culture, processes, and objectives. Their unique contributions are often instrumental in driving the organization's strategic initiatives and achieving its goals.

In essence, by focusing on the internal development of human capital, firms can ensure that they are leveraging the full potential of their workforce. Employees with valuable and unique skills become integral to the organization's success, serving as a critical source of competitive advantage. Their specialized abilities are not easily replicated, which makes them indispensable assets to the organization.

In summary, human capital that is both valuable and unique represents a key differentiator for organizations. The decision to develop such skills internally rather than relying on external sources reflects a strategic approach to maximizing the value created by employees. These organization-specific skills, developed through targeted investment, enable firms to gain and sustain a competitive edge in the marketplace. Core employees with these unique skills are essential not only for their immediate contributions but also for their long-term impact on the organization's success and strategic positioning.

Acquiring Human Capital

Human capital is valuable, yet widely available throughout the labor market. Because these skills are valuable, organizations have an incentive to internalize employment. However, since skills in this quadrant are not unique or specific to a firm, human capital partners would suggest that managers may be hesitant to invest in internal development Employees with generic skills may leave and transfer the organization's investment to another firm.

Organizations may reconcile these conflicting pressures by acquiring (i.e., buying) human capital from the market that does not require further investment. An acquisition mode enables firms to reap the benefits of valuable skills that have been developed elsewhere while holding them internally. In so doing, the acquiring firm simply pays the value reflected in the market price and realizes immediate benefits vis-a-vis productivity.

Selecting skilled employees directly from the market may also allow firms to realize significant savings in developmental expenditures while gaining instant access to a wide variety of capabilities that may incur positive returns on investment.

Human capital, while highly valuable, is often widely available in the labor market. This broad availability can create a complex situation for organizations. On one hand, the value of such skills provides a strong incentive for firms to hire these employees internally rather than seeking to outsource or utilize external sources. However, the generic nature of these skills—meaning they are not unique or specific to any one organization—can present challenges. Managers might be reluctant to invest heavily in the internal development of employees with such skills because these individuals may leave the organization, taking with them the firm's investment and potentially contributing to competitors instead.

To address this dilemma, organizations might choose to acquire human capital through external means rather than developing it internally. This approach involves purchasing skilled employees from the labor market who have already acquired valuable competencies elsewhere. By adopting this acquisition strategy, firms can benefit from the expertise and capabilities that these employees bring without needing to invest in their initial development. Essentially, the firm pays the market value for these skills and gains immediate advantages in terms of productivity and performance.

This acquisition mode presents several benefits. Firstly, it allows organizations to bypass the costs and time associated with developing skills in-house. By hiring individuals who have already honed their abilities in different settings, firms can save on developmental expenditures and avoid the risks associated with investing in employees who might not remain with the company for the long term.

Additionally, acquiring skilled employees from the market provides firms with instant access to a diverse range of capabilities. This immediate access can lead to a rapid return on investment, as the newly hired employees can start contributing to the organization's goals and operations almost immediately. The firm benefits from their pre-existing skills and experience, which can enhance overall productivity and drive positive outcomes.

In summary, while human capital with valuable but generic skills is broadly available, organizations face a choice between developing these skills internally or acquiring them from the market. The decision to acquire human capital rather than invest in its internal development allows firms to leverage valuable skills without the associated risks of employee turnover and investment loss. By purchasing skilled employees who have already been trained elsewhere, firms can achieve significant cost savings and gain quick access to a range of capabilities that contribute to their success and productivity.

Contracting Human Capital

Human capital that is generic and of limited strategic value. Skills that can be purchased easily on the open labor market and, therefore, can be treated essentially as a commodity. The limited uniqueness of these skills provides a disincentive for firms to invest significant resources toward employee development. fact,

Because so many alternative sources for these skills exist, firms may decrease employment costs by contracting externally.

As the supply of qualified suppliers increases and the risk inherent in contractual arrangements decreases, organizations can contract work without jeopardizing their competitive position.

Although many contractual relationships stipulate that the actual work be done off company premises (and only the product of that labor will be traded), it is increasingly common that contractual work is performed on-site. Temporary employees, leasing arrangements, and other forms of contract work often fall within this category.

Human capital consisting of generic skills with limited strategic value represents a category of talent that is readily available and can be easily procured from the open labor market. These skills are often seen as commodities because they are not unique or specialized to any particular organization. As a result, firms face little incentive to invest heavily in the internal development of employees possessing such skills. Since these competencies can be acquired with relative ease from various external sources, investing significant resources in their enhancement becomes less appealing.

The abundance of available talent with these generic skills allows organizations to reduce employment costs by opting for external contracting rather than internal development. Firms can leverage external suppliers or contractors to fulfill their needs without bearing the expense and risk associated with training and developing these skills in-house. This approach helps organizations manage their operational costs more effectively while ensuring they have access to the necessary skills.

As the pool of qualified suppliers grows and the risks associated with contractual arrangements decrease, firms find it increasingly viable to contract work externally. This shift allows organizations to access skilled labor without the commitment of long-term employment, which can be particularly advantageous when dealing with skills that do not provide a significant strategic advantage. The flexibility to outsource tasks reduces the burden on internal resources and minimizes the need for substantial investment in employee development.

Contractual relationships involving generic skills often stipulate that the work be performed off company premises, with the organization only paying for the end product or service. However, it is becoming more common for such work to be conducted on-site, reflecting a trend towards greater integration of external talent within the organization's operational environment. Temporary employees, leasing arrangements, and other forms of contract work frequently fall into this category, providing firms with the ability to manage labor costs while still maintaining access to necessary skills.

In essence, when human capital comprises generic skills that are widely available and lack unique strategic value, organizations are motivated to pursue external contracting options. This strategy allows them to capitalize on the efficiency and cost-effectiveness of acquiring skills from the market without the investment risks associated with internal development. By utilizing temporary or contracted labor, firms can meet their operational needs and optimize their resource allocation, all while safeguarding their competitive position and ensuring that their labor costs remain manageable.

Creating Human Capital Alliances

Human capital is unique in some way but not directly instrumental in creating customer value. Given its uniqueness, this form of human capital might, at first glance, appear to be optimized through internal development.

Given the limited value-creating potential, minimal benefit may be gained from outright ownership of these types of skills.

Some unique forms of human capital are less codified and transferable than generic skills, yet more widely available than firm-specific skills. In these cases organizations face a paradox; they are simultaneously encouraged to use external and internal employment modes. If outright internalization is prohibitive from a cost/benefit standpoint and complete contracting involves risks of opportunism, some form of alliance between parties may provide a hybrid employment mode that blends internalization and externalization and overcomes these problems.

Alliance to refer to an external relationship where each party con – tributes to a jointly shared outcome.

Human capital that exhibits unique characteristics but is not directly instrumental in creating customer value represents a complex asset for organizations. This type of human capital may initially seem ideal for internal development due to its distinctiveness, which suggests that its potential could be best realized within the organization. However, despite its uniqueness, these skills may not substantially contribute to immediate value creation for customers, which affects the overall cost-benefit analysis of internal development.

While unique human capital may not be as widely available as generic skills, it is often more accessible than highly specialized, firm-specific skills. This availability creates a paradox for organizations. On one hand, the distinct nature of these skills could justify investing in their internal development. On the other hand, if these skills do not directly enhance customer value, the investment in developing and maintaining them may not yield significant returns.

Given this paradox, organizations must navigate the tension between internal development and external contracting. Internalizing these unique skills can be cost-prohibitive, especially if the benefits of having these skills in-house are limited. Conversely, complete external contracting might involve risks such as opportunism, where external partners could exploit the organization's reliance on their unique skills or fail to deliver as expected.

To address these challenges, organizations often turn to hybrid employment models, such as strategic alliances, which blend elements of both internalization and externalization. An alliance involves forming a partnership with an external entity where both parties contribute to and share in the outcomes of the collaboration. This approach allows organizations to leverage the unique skills of external partners while maintaining some level of control and oversight.

Through alliances, organizations can mitigate the risks associated with contracting out unique skills while avoiding the full costs of internal development. This hybrid model facilitates access to specialized knowledge and capabilities without the need for substantial internal investment. It also enables organizations to benefit from external expertise while aligning these benefits with their strategic objectives and ensuring that both parties are incentivized to contribute to the shared outcome.

When dealing with human capital that is unique but not directly tied to customer value, organizations face a challenging decision between internal development and external contracting. A hybrid approach, such as forming strategic alliances, can offer a practical solution by combining the strengths of both models. By engaging in alliances, organizations can access valuable, unique skills and share the benefits and risks associated with these capabilities, optimizing their overall human capital strategy while addressing cost and control concerns.

CHAPTER 2

ORGANIZATION STRUCTURE

Question

With a clear understanding of which resources to hire externally and which to develop internally, as well as insights into building an effective team based on the HR Architecture framework, we now move to the next critical step: organizing the team into a coherent structure. This stage is essential for ensuring that the team functions efficiently and aligns with the organization's strategic goals.

Organizing the Team into a Structure:

Define Clear Roles and Responsibilities: The first step in organizing a team is to clearly define the roles and responsibilities of each team member. This involves creating detailed job descriptions that outline the specific duties, expectations, and performance criteria for each position. Clear roles help prevent overlap and confusion, ensuring that every team member understands their contribution to the team's overall objectives.

Establish Reporting Lines: Effective team organization requires a well-defined reporting structure. Determine who will report to whom, and establish a hierarchy that reflects the organization's structure and operational needs. This hierarchy should facilitate communication and decision-making processes. It is crucial to create an organizational chart that visually represents this structure, making it easier for team members to understand their reporting relationships and the chain of command.

Promote Effective Communication Channels: Communication is a key component of a well-organized team. Establish channels and protocols for both formal and informal communication. This includes setting up regular meetings, reporting systems, and feedback mechanisms. Effective communication ensures that information flows seamlessly throughout the team, enabling collaboration and prompt resolution of issues.

Foster Collaboration and Team Dynamics: Organizing a team also involves fostering a collaborative environment. Encourage teamwork by creating opportunities for team members to work together on projects, share knowledge, and support each other. Team-building activities and collaborative tools can help enhance team dynamics and build trust among team members.

Implement a Performance Management System: To ensure that the team is aligned with organizational goals, implement a performance management system. This system should include regular performance evaluations, goal-setting processes, and feedback mechanisms. By monitoring and assessing performance, you can identify areas for improvement, recognize achievements, and make informed decisions about development and career progression.

Allocate Resources and Manage Workload: Efficient team organization involves appropriate allocation of resources and management of workloads. Ensure that each team member has the necessary tools, support, and training to perform their role effectively. Monitor workloads to prevent overburdening team members and adjust resource allocation as needed to maintain balance and productivity.

Adapt to Changes and Evolving Needs: An effective team structure should be flexible and adaptable to changes. As the organization grows and evolves, be prepared to reassess and adjust the team structure to meet new demands and challenges. This may involve reorganizing teams, redefining roles, or introducing new processes to ensure continued alignment with organizational objectives.

Support Development and Growth: Finally, support the ongoing development and growth of your team members. Provide opportunities for professional development, training, and career advancement. Investing in the growth of your team not only enhances their skills but also contributes to overall team effectiveness and satisfaction.

By carefully organizing your team using these principles, you can create a structured and efficient work environment that supports your organization's goals and enhances team performance. This approach ensures that each team member's skills and roles are optimized, leading to a more cohesive and productive team.

Aligning structure with strategy

Achieving profitable performance within an organization hinge on the effective alignment of four critical business elements. These elements—leadership, organization, jobs, and people—must work cohesively to ensure the successful development, execution, and monitoring of the organization's strategy.

Leadership: Leadership is central to steering the organization toward its strategic goals. It involves the individuals who are tasked with crafting and deploying the strategic vision, as well as overseeing its implementation and assessing outcomes. Effective leaders are responsible for setting the direction, making strategic decisions, and ensuring that the entire organization is focused on achieving its objectives. Their ability to inspire, guide, and adjust the strategy based on performance metrics is crucial for maintaining alignment and driving profitable results.

Organization: The organizational structure, processes, and operations play a pivotal role in how the strategy is executed. This element encompasses the design of the organization's framework, including its hierarchy, communication channels, and workflow systems. A well-organized structure facilitates efficient strategy deployment by ensuring that processes are streamlined and operations are effective. The alignment of organizational processes with strategic goals ensures that resources are utilized optimally and that the organization can adapt to changing circumstances while maintaining focus on its strategic objectives.

Jobs: Jobs define the specific roles and responsibilities required to implement the strategy effectively. This element involves identifying and defining the necessary positions, tasks, and accountabilities that support strategic execution. Each job must be aligned with the organization's goals, ensuring that every role contributes to the overarching strategy. Clearly defined roles help prevent overlaps, gaps, and inefficiencies, making it easier for teams to work together towards common objectives.

People: The success of strategy execution largely depends on the people within the organization. This element focuses on the experience, skills, and competencies required to perform the roles effectively. It involves ensuring that the right individuals are in place, equipped with the necessary qualifications and capabilities to execute the strategy. Talent management, including recruitment, training, and development, is crucial for building a workforce that can meet the demands of the strategy and adapt to evolving needs.

For an organization to achieve profitable performance, these four elements must be aligned and integrated seamlessly. Leadership must drive the strategic vision and oversee its implementation through an appropriately structured organization. The organizational framework must support well-defined jobs, with each role clearly contributing to the strategic objectives. Furthermore, the people within the organization must possess the requisite skills and competencies to execute their roles effectively.

The alignment of leadership, organization, jobs, and people is essential for achieving profitable performance. Each element must support and reinforce the others to ensure that the strategy is not only well-developed but also effectively executed and continuously improved. This alignment facilitates efficient operations, maximizes the use of resources, and drives the organization towards its strategic goals, ultimately leading to enhanced profitability and long-term success.

Key elements of organization structure

Organizational structure is a critical framework that defines how activities are coordinated and managed within an organization. It establishes the relationships and hierarchies that facilitate the efficient execution of tasks and the achievement of strategic goals. Five fundamental elements that create and shape an organizational structure are:

Job Design: Job design refers to the process of defining the roles and responsibilities of employees within the organization. It involves specifying the tasks, duties, and expectations associated with each position to ensure that they align with the organization's objectives and strategy. Effective job design enhances job satisfaction, productivity, and efficiency by ensuring that roles are well-structured and that employees understand their responsibilities. It also involves considering factors such as job rotation, task variety, and autonomy to optimize performance and engagement.

Departmentation: Departmentation is the process of dividing the organization into distinct units or departments based on various criteria such as function, product, geography, or customer type. This element of organizational structure helps to organize activities and resources in a way that improves specialization and efficiency. By grouping similar functions or activities together, departmentation allows for clearer lines of authority, better coordination, and more focused expertise. For example, a company might have separate departments for marketing, finance, and human resources to streamline operations and enhance functional effectiveness.

Delegation: Delegation involves the assignment of authority and responsibility from higher levels of management to lower levels within the organization. It is a crucial aspect of organizational structure as it determines how tasks and decision-making are distributed across various levels. Effective delegation ensures that decision-making is decentralized, empowering employees at different levels to take ownership of their tasks and contribute to the organization's goals. It also helps in developing employee skills and optimizing managerial efficiency by allowing managers to focus on higher-level strategic issues.

Span of Control: Span of control refers to the number of subordinates that a manager or supervisor can effectively oversee and manage. This element impacts the organization's hierarchy and structure by determining the breadth of supervision and the number of levels in the organizational hierarchy. A narrow span of control means that a manager supervises a small number of employees, which can lead to a more hierarchical structure with more levels of management. Conversely, a wide span of control means that a manager oversees a larger group, which can lead to a flatter organizational structure with fewer management levels. The appropriate span of control depends on factors such as the nature of the tasks, the complexity of the work, and the managerial capabilities.

Chain of Command: The chain of command defines the line of authority and communication within an organization. It specifies who reports to whom and the hierarchical levels through which decisions and instructions flow. This element ensures clarity in reporting relationships and accountability, facilitating the efficient execution of tasks and the resolution of issues. A well-defined chain of command helps to maintain order, avoid confusion, and ensure that everyone understands their role and the appropriate channels for communication and decision-making.

In summary, the organizational structure is shaped by the interplay of these five elements: job design, departmentation, delegation, span of control, and chain of command. Each element plays a crucial role in defining how work is organized, managed, and executed within the organization. By carefully designing and integrating these components, organizations can enhance their efficiency, clarity, and effectiveness, ultimately contributing to their overall success and strategic objectives.

Types of organization structure

1. Vertical—functional and divisional.
2. Vertical and horizontal matrix.
3. Boundary-less ("open boundary") – modular, virtual, and cellular.

Vertical structure

Two main types of vertical structure exist, functional and divisional. The functional structure divides work and employees by specialization. It is a hierarchical, usually vertically integrated, structure. It emphasizes standardization in organization and processes for specialized employees in relatively narrow jobs. This traditional type of organization forms departments such as production, sales, research and development, accounting, HR, and marketing. Each department has a separate function and specializes in that area. For example, all HR professionals are part of the same function and report to a senior leader of HR. The same reporting process would be true for other functions, such as finance or operations. In functional structures, employees report directly to managers within their functional areas who in turn report to a chief officer of the organization. Management from above must centrally coordinate the specialized departments.

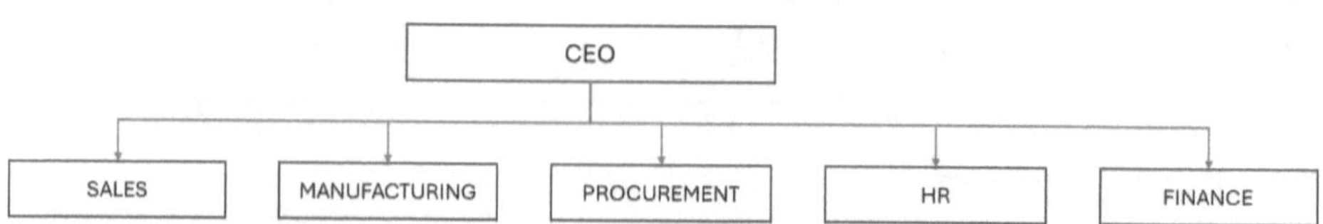

Figure 2: Vertical Organizational Structure (functional)

Also, a vertical arrangement, a divisional structure most often divides work and employees by output, although a divisional structure could be divided by another variable such as market or region. For example, a business that sells men's, women's, and children's clothing through retail, e-commerce, and catalog sales in the Northeast, Southeast, and Southwest could be using a divisional structure in one of three ways:

1. Product—men's wear, women's wear, and children's clothing.
2. Market—retail store, e-commerce, and catalog.
3. Region—Northeast, Southeast, and Southwest.

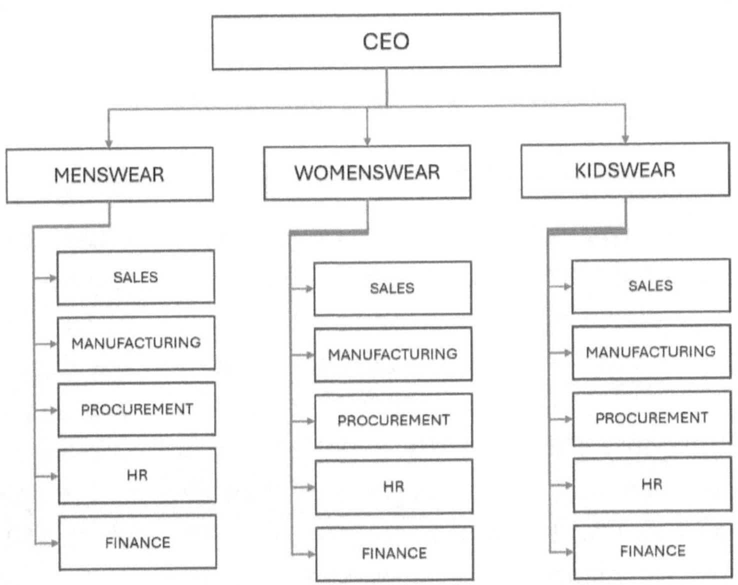

Figure 3: Vertical Organizational Structure (divisional)

Matrix Organizational Structure

A matrix structure combines the functional and divisional structures to create a dual-command situation. In a matrix structure, an employee reports to two managers who are jointly responsible for the employee's performance. Typically, one manager works in an administrative function, such as finance, HR, information technology, sales or marketing, and the other works in a business unit related to a product, service, customer or geography.

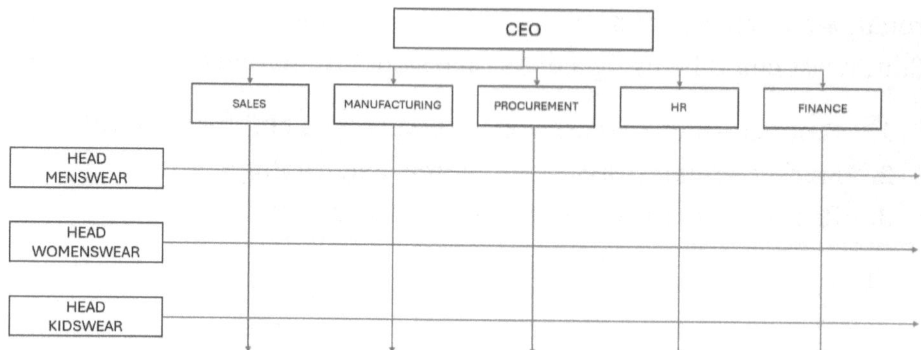

Figure 4: Matrix Organizational Structure

Open boundary organization structure

More recent trends in structural forms remove the traditional boundaries of an organization. Typical internal and external barriers and organizational boxes are eliminated, and all organizational units are effectively and flexibly connected. Teams replace departments, and the organization and suppliers work as closely together as parts of one company. The hierarchy is flat; status and rank are minimal. Everyone—including top management, managers and employees— participates in the decision-making process. The use of 360-degree feedback performance appraisals is common as well.

The Impact of Growth Stages on Organizational Structure

Organizations typically progress through a series of predictable stages as they mature, each stage presenting unique challenges and requiring adjustments in structure, management, and priorities. Understanding these stages helps in effectively navigating growth and optimizing performance. The four key stages of an organization's life cycle are:

Startup

In the startup phase, organizations are in their infancy, marked by a period of initial development and experimentation. At this stage, growth is often inconsistent and unpredictable, as the organization is still finding its footing and establishing its market presence. The organizational structure is usually simple and informal, reflecting the nascent nature of the business. Decision-making tends to be highly centralized, with founders or a small leadership team making most of the key decisions. This centralization helps in maintaining control and quickly addressing issues as they arise.

Startups often operate with minimal formal systems and processes, relying on informal communication and ad-hoc methods to manage operations. The focus is on innovation and establishing a viable business model. Examples of organizations in this stage include many "dotcom" companies during the early days of the internet boom, where rapid experimentation and pivoting were common.

Expansion

As organizations transition to the expansion stage, they experience rapid and positive growth, which brings about the need for more structured systems and processes. This period is characterized by the establishment of formal systems to handle increased complexity and scale. Despite this growth, many organizations at this stage continue to emphasize centralization, with decision-making remaining largely within the upper echelons of management.

During expansion, the organization focuses on scaling its operations, enhancing efficiency, and solidifying its market position. While formal systems are introduced to manage increased demands, delegation is often still limited, as the leadership team seeks to maintain control and ensure consistent implementation of the strategy across the expanding organization.

Consolidation

In the consolidation stage, organizations experience a shift from rapid growth to more stable and controlled expansion. Growth rates slow down, and the organization becomes more structured. Departmentalization becomes prominent, with distinct functional areas or divisions being established to handle various aspects of the business. Formalized systems and processes are further developed to support this increased complexity.

Centralization tends to be moderate in the consolidation stage, as the organization balances between maintaining control and allowing for more localized decision-making. This stage is marked by a focus on efficiency, process improvement, and optimizing the performance of existing operations. The organization works to consolidate its gains and ensure sustainable growth.

Diversification

The diversification stage occurs when older, larger organizations seek to expand into new markets or product lines, often leading to significant organizational changes. This phase is characterized by rapid growth through diversification, which can introduce increased complexity and necessitate a shift toward more bureaucratic structures. Decentralization becomes more pronounced, as the organization needs to manage a wider array of activities and geographic locations.

Bureaucracy and formal processes become more entrenched to handle the complexities of diverse operations. Decision-making is distributed across various divisions or business units, allowing for more localized management and adaptation to different market conditions. The organization must balance the benefits of decentralization with the need for coherence and coordination across its diverse activities.

As organizations progress through the stages of startup, expansion, consolidation, and diversification, they encounter different challenges and demands that necessitate changes in their structure, management practices, and priorities. Each stage requires tailored approaches to effectively manage growth and maintain organizational effectiveness, ensuring that the organization can adapt and thrive through its evolving life cycle.

Structural dimensions

Leaders seeking to gain insight into their organization's internal environment can benefit greatly from measuring and analyzing various structural dimensions. These dimensions help in understanding how the organization operates and how its structure supports or hinders its strategic goals. Typically assessed through surveys or organizational assessments, these key dimensions include:

Specialization

Specialization refers to the extent to which an organization's activities are divided into specialized roles or functions. This dimension gauges how tasks and responsibilities are distributed among employees and departments. High specialization means that employees have clearly defined, narrowly focused roles, which can lead to increased efficiency and expertise in specific areas. However, it can also result in siloed departments and potential communication challenges. Understanding specialization helps leaders assess whether the organization's structure supports efficient task execution and if roles are appropriately aligned with strategic objectives.

Standardization

Standardization measures the degree to which an organization operates under standardized rules, procedures, and practices. It reflects how uniformity is maintained across different functions and locations within the organization. High standardization implies that there are established protocols and procedures that guide operations, ensuring consistency and predictability. While this can enhance efficiency and quality control, it may also limit flexibility and responsiveness. Evaluating standardization helps leaders determine whether existing procedures are adequate for maintaining operational consistency and if there is a need for more or less formal control.

Formalization

Formalization assesses the extent to which instructions, procedures, and guidelines are documented and codified. This dimension focuses on the level of written documentation available to employees, which can include policies, manuals, and standard operating procedures. High formalization indicates that the organization has well-defined processes and clear documentation, which supports consistency and compliance. Conversely, low formalization may suggest more informal processes that could lead to variability in performance and decision-making. Leaders use this dimension to evaluate whether documentation supports effective and efficient operations or if more formal structures are needed.

Centralization

Centralization refers to the degree to which decision-making authority is concentrated at the top levels of the management hierarchy. In a centralized organization, key decisions are made by top executives or a central authority, which can lead to uniform decision-making and control. On the other hand, decentralization spreads decision-making authority throughout various levels, allowing for more localized and potentially faster responses. Assessing centralization helps leaders understand how decisions are made within the organization and whether the current level of centralization supports or impedes strategic objectives and operational efficiency.

Configuration

Configuration encompasses the overall shape and structure of the organization's role hierarchy and reporting relationships. It includes several components:

Chain of Command: This dimension measures the number of vertical levels or layers in the organizational hierarchy. A longer chain of command indicates more layers between top executives and frontline employees, which can affect communication and decision-making speed. A shorter chain of command typically results in a flatter organization with fewer hierarchical levels.

Span of Control: Span of control refers to the number of direct reports per manager or the number of horizontal layers in the organizational structure. A narrow span of control means that managers oversee fewer employees, which can lead to more direct supervision but potentially more managerial layers. A wide span of control indicates that managers supervise more employees, which can enhance autonomy but might strain managerial oversight.

Understanding these aspects of organizational configuration helps leaders evaluate how effectively the organizational structure supports communication, decision-making, and operational efficiency. It also aids in identifying areas where structural adjustments may be needed to better align with strategic goals and improve overall performance.

By measuring and analyzing these structural dimensions—specialization, standardization, formalization, centralization, and configuration—leaders can develop a comprehensive understanding of their organization's internal environment. This insight enables them to make informed decisions about structural adjustments and management practices that enhance organizational effectiveness and support strategic objectives.

Contextual Factors

To gain a comprehensive understanding of an organization's external environment and how it interacts with its internal dynamics, it is crucial to review various contextual factors. These factors provide insights into the organization's origins, structure, operational scale, and external dependencies, all of which impact its strategic positioning and effectiveness. Here are some significant contextual factors to consider:

Origin and History

Examining the origin and history of an organization offers valuable insights into its foundational principles and evolution over time. Key questions to consider include:

Was the organization privately founded or established through other means? Understanding whether it started as a private entity, a public venture, or through mergers and acquisitions helps clarify its initial strategic objectives and growth trajectory.

What changes have occurred in ownership or location? Tracking changes in ownership, such as transitions from private to public status or shifts in control, can reveal how these transitions have influenced organizational strategies and operations. Additionally, changes in location or expansion into new markets often reflect strategic adjustments in response to evolving opportunities and challenges.

Ownership and Control

Ownership and control are critical in determining the governance structure and strategic direction of the organization. Important considerations include:

Is the organization private or public? This distinction affects regulatory requirements, access to capital, and transparency. Private organizations may have more flexibility in decision-making, while public organizations must adhere to stricter disclosure and governance standards.

Is control divided among a few individuals or many? Understanding the concentration or dispersion of control helps gauge decision-making dynamics and potential influences on organizational strategy. Centralized control by a few individuals might streamline decision-making but could limit diverse perspectives, whereas distributed control may enhance inclusiveness but slow down decision-making processes.

Size

The size of an organization significantly impacts its operational capacity and market presence. Key metrics to evaluate include:

Number of employees: This provides an indication of the organization's scale and its capacity to manage and execute various functions.

Net assets: Assessing net assets helps determine the financial strength and resource availability of the organization.

Market position: Evaluating market position involves understanding the organization's competitive standing, market share, and overall influence within its industry. Size and market position often correlate, influencing strategic decisions and growth opportunities.

Location

Location is a crucial factor that affects operational efficiency and market accessibility. Considerations include:

Number of operating sites: The extent and distribution of operating sites, including headquarters, branch offices, and production facilities, can impact logistics, regional market reach, and overall operational complexity. A widespread location network might support global reach and market penetration, while a concentrated location might enhance focus and control.

Products and Services

The nature of the products and services offered by the organization defines its market niche and competitive advantage. Key questions to explore include:

What types of goods and services does the organization manufacture and provide? Understanding the range and scope of products or services helps identify the organization's core competencies, market focus, and value propositions. It also highlights potential areas for innovation, differentiation, and strategic development.

Technology

Technology integration is essential for operational efficiency and competitive advantage. Important aspects include:

Are the organization's work processes effectively integrated? Evaluating how well technology supports and integrates with work processes helps assess operational effectiveness, productivity, and innovation capabilities. Effective integration of technology can streamline operations, enhance data management, and facilitate better decision-making.

Interdependence

The degree of interdependence with external entities affects organizational stability and strategy. Consider:

What is the degree to which the organization depends on customers, suppliers, trade unions, or other related entities? Understanding these dependencies helps identify potential risks and opportunities in the supply chain, customer relationships, and labor relations. High interdependence may require robust management strategies to mitigate risks and leverage collaborative opportunities.

Reviewing these contextual factors—origin and history, ownership and control, size, location, products and services, technology, and interdependence—provides a comprehensive understanding of the organization's external environment and its interplay with internal dynamics. This analysis is essential for making informed strategic decisions, anticipating challenges, and capitalizing on opportunities in the ever-evolving business landscape.

Example of an Organization Structure

When building an organizational structure for a startup in the IT sector, it is essential to focus on three fundamental pillars: career levels, capabilities or skills, and team or departmental alignment. These pillars will help ensure that the structure supports both operational efficiency and strategic growth. Here's how to approach each pillar:

Career Levels

Career levels define the hierarchical structure and progression paths within the organization. They help establish clear roles and responsibilities, provide a framework for career development, and guide recruitment and promotion practices. For an IT startup, career levels typically include:

Entry-Level Positions: These roles are for individuals who are starting their careers or transitioning into IT. Common titles might include Junior Developer, IT Support Specialist, or Systems Analyst. These positions focus on foundational tasks and learning.

Mid-Level Positions: Employees at this level have gained experience and are responsible for more complex tasks. Titles may include Software Engineer, Network Administrator, or Project Manager. They are expected to handle significant projects, lead small teams, and contribute to strategic planning.

Senior-Level Positions: These roles involve leadership and strategic oversight. Titles such as Senior Developer, IT Manager, or Lead Architect fall into this category. Senior-level employees oversee major projects, mentor junior staff, and influence organizational strategy.

Executive-Level Positions: The top tier includes roles like Chief Technology Officer (CTO), Chief Information Officer (CIO), or Vice President of IT. These leaders are responsible for setting the strategic direction of the IT department, making high-level decisions, and ensuring alignment with overall business goals.

Capabilities or Skills

Capabilities or skills are crucial for defining the functional expertise required at each career level. They ensure that employees have the necessary qualifications and competencies to perform their roles effectively. For an IT startup, essential skills might include:

Technical Skills: These include programming languages (e.g., Python, Java), software development, systems integration, cybersecurity, and data management. Technical skills vary depending on the role, from basic coding to advanced system design and network security.

Project Management: Skills in project management are vital for ensuring that IT projects are completed on time and within budget. This includes knowledge of project management methodologies (e.g., Agile, Scrum), planning, resource allocation, risk management, and stakeholder communication.

Problem-Solving and Analytical Skills: Employees should possess strong problem-solving abilities to address technical challenges, troubleshoot issues, and implement effective solutions. Analytical skills are necessary for interpreting data, making informed decisions, and optimizing processes.

Communication and Collaboration: Effective communication skills are crucial for coordinating with team members, clients, and stakeholders. Collaboration skills ensure that team members can work together efficiently, share knowledge, and achieve common goals.

Leadership and Management: For higher career levels, leadership and management skills are important for guiding teams, setting strategic objectives, and managing organizational change. This includes people management, strategic planning, and decision-making.

Team or Departmental Alignment

Team or departmental alignment involves organizing employees into functional groups that support the startup's objectives and workflows. It helps in streamlining operations and clarifying reporting relationships. For an IT startup, typical departments or teams might include:

Development Team: Responsible for software development, including front-end and back-end development, database management, and quality assurance. This team focuses on building and maintaining technology products.

IT Support and Operations: Handles day-to-day IT support, infrastructure maintenance, and system administration. This team ensures that IT systems are functioning smoothly and addresses any technical issues that arise.

Project Management Office (PMO): Oversees project planning, execution, and monitoring. This team ensures that IT projects are delivered successfully, adhering to timelines and budgets.

Product Management: Focuses on defining product requirements, managing product lifecycles, and aligning product development with market needs. This team works closely with both the development and marketing teams.

Sales and Marketing: Responsible for promoting IT products or services, generating leads, and managing customer relationships. This team drives business growth through effective sales strategies and marketing campaigns.

Research and Development (R&D): Engages in innovation and the development of new technologies or solutions. This team explores emerging trends and develops cutting-edge products or features.

Putting It All Together

To build an effective organizational structure for your IT startup, integrate these three pillars:

Defining clear career levels with corresponding roles and responsibilities.

Identifying and developing essential capabilities or skills required at each level.

Aligning employees into well-defined teams or departments to support operational needs and strategic goals.

By addressing these pillars, you can create a structured, efficient, and dynamic organization that supports growth, fosters innovation, and drives success in the competitive IT landscape.

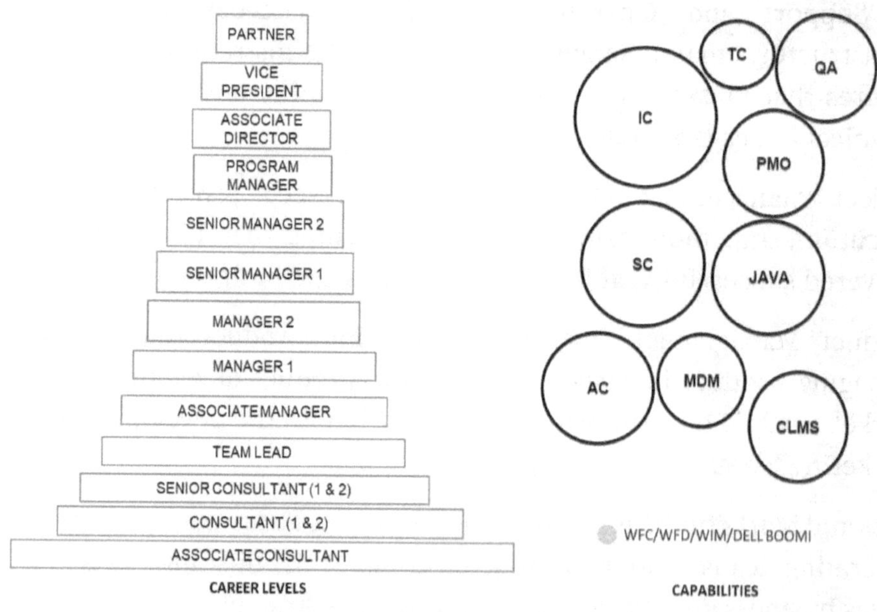

Figure 5: Career Framework

(*Abbreviations: IC:* **Integration** *Consultant. TC: Technical Consultant. etc.*)

CHAPTER 3

ORGANIZATIONAL CULTURE

Question

Having established how to build a team and design an organizational structure, the next crucial step is defining the type of organizational culture you wish to foster within the company. Organizational culture encompasses the values, beliefs, and behaviors that shape how employees interact and work together. It is a fundamental element that influences how you engage with your team, monitor their performance, manage their development, and ensure alignment with the company's mission and values.

Understanding and Defining Organizational Culture

Articulate Core Values and Vision: Start by clearly articulating the core values and vision of the organization. These should reflect the fundamental principles and aspirations of the company. Core values serve as a guide for expected behaviors and decision-making processes, while the vision provides a long-term perspective on what the company aims to achieve. Communicating these elements effectively helps to set the tone for the organizational culture.

Define Desired Cultural Attributes: Identify the specific cultural attributes that you want to nurture within the organization. This might include traits such as innovation, collaboration, integrity, or customer focus. Defining these attributes helps to create a clear picture of the type of culture you want to develop and provides a benchmark for evaluating whether the culture is being upheld.

Develop Cultural Norms and Practices: Establish norms and practices that reinforce the desired organizational culture. This includes designing policies, procedures, and rituals that reflect and support the cultural values. For instance, if teamwork is a key cultural attribute, you might implement collaborative workspaces, regular team-building activities, and cross-functional projects.

Engage and Communicate with Your Team: Effective communication is crucial in embedding organizational culture. Regularly engage with your team to reinforce cultural values through meetings, workshops, and internal communications. Use stories, examples, and leadership actions to illustrate and celebrate behaviors that align with the desired culture.

Monitor and Evaluate Cultural Alignment: To ensure that the organizational culture is being embraced, implement mechanisms for monitoring and evaluating cultural alignment. This can include employee surveys, feedback sessions, and performance reviews. Assess how well team members are adhering to the cultural norms and identify areas where additional support or adjustments may be needed.

Provide Leadership and Role Modeling: Leadership plays a pivotal role in shaping and maintaining organizational culture. Leaders should model the behaviors and values that reflect the desired culture. By demonstrating commitment to cultural values through their actions and decisions, leaders set a standard for others to follow.

Manage and Support Team Members: Use the organizational culture as a framework for managing and supporting your team. This involves providing guidance, coaching, and feedback that align with cultural expectations. Ensure that performance management practices, such as goal-setting and evaluations, reflect cultural values and encourage behaviors that support the desired culture.

Align Recruitment and Onboarding: Incorporate cultural considerations into recruitment and onboarding processes. Select candidates whose values and behaviors align with the organizational culture, and provide new hires with orientation and training that emphasize cultural norms and expectations. This helps to ensure that new team members integrate smoothly into the cultural framework of the organization.

Promote Continuous Improvement: Organizational culture is not static; it evolves over time. Encourage continuous improvement by regularly revisiting and refining cultural practices and norms. Solicit feedback from employees and be open to making changes that enhance the alignment between culture and organizational goals.

Celebrate Cultural Successes: Recognize and celebrate achievements that exemplify the organizational culture. Acknowledge and reward team members who demonstrate cultural values in their work. Celebrations and recognitions reinforce the importance of the culture and motivate others to follow suit.

By understanding and defining the organizational culture you want to create, you can effectively engage with your team, manage their performance, and ensure alignment with your company's values and objectives. A well-defined culture not only enhances team cohesion and satisfaction but also drives the organization toward its strategic goals.

Culture types

Organizational culture is shaped by various underlying assumptions and values that guide employee behavior and influence overall effectiveness. Four distinct cultural archetypes provide different approaches to managing and motivating people. These are the Clan, Adhocracy, Market, and Hierarchy cultures. Each has unique assumptions, values, expected behaviors, and methods for monitoring effectiveness. Here's an overview of each:

Clan Culture

Assumption: Human Affiliation

In a Clan culture, the emphasis is on creating a strong sense of belonging and interpersonal relationships within the organization. The underlying belief is that people perform best when they feel trust, loyalty, and a sense of community.

Values

- Attachment
- Affiliation
- Collaboration
- Trust
- Support

Expected Behaviors

- Teamwork: Employees work together harmoniously to achieve common goals.
- Participation: Involvement in decision-making processes and organizational activities is encouraged.
- Employee Involvement: Active engagement and contribution of ideas from all levels are promoted.
- Open Communication: Transparent and frequent communication channels are maintained to foster trust and collaboration.

Monitoring Effectiveness

- Employee Satisfaction: Regular assessments of employee contentment with their roles and the organizational environment.
- Commitment: Evaluation of employees' dedication to the organization and its goals.

Adhocracy Culture

Assumption: Change

An Adhocracy culture thrives on innovation and flexibility. It is founded on the belief that individuals perform optimally when they understand the significance of their tasks and are empowered to act creatively.

Values

- Growth
- Stimulation
- Variety
- Autonomy
- Attention to Detail

Expected Behaviors

- Risk-Taking: Encouragement of experimentation and willingness to take calculated risks.
- Creativity: Promotion of innovative thinking and problem-solving.
- Adaptability: Ability to swiftly adjust to changing conditions and new challenges.
- *Monitoring Effectiveness*
- Innovation: Measurement of the organization's capacity to introduce new ideas, products, or processes and its impact on the market.

Market Culture

Assumption: Achievement

In a Market culture, the focus is on performance and results. It is predicated on the belief that employees are motivated by clear objectives and rewards based on their accomplishments.

Values

- Communication
- Competition
- Competence
- Achievement

Expected Behaviors

- Gathering Information: Collecting data on customer needs and competitor activities to inform strategies.
- Goal Setting: Establishing clear, measurable objectives for performance.
- Planning Task Focus: Prioritizing tasks that align with strategic goals and market demands.
- Competitiveness: Striving to outperform rivals and achieve superior market position.
- Aggressiveness: Proactive pursuit of business opportunities and challenges.

Monitoring Effectiveness

- Market Share: Tracking the organization's share of the market relative to competitors.
- Profit: Evaluating financial performance and profitability.
- Product Quality: Assessing the standard of products or services offered.
- Productivity: Measuring efficiency in achieving business objectives.

Hierarchy Culture

Assumption: Human Stability

A Hierarchy culture values stability and order. It is based on the belief that employees thrive in environments with clearly defined roles and formal procedures.

Values

- Communication
- Routinization
- Formalization

Expected Behaviors

- Conformity: Adherence to established procedures and norms.
- Predictability: Consistent and reliable performance through standardized processes.
- *Monitoring Effectiveness*
- Efficiency: Assessing how well the organization utilizes resources to achieve its goals.
- Timeliness: Evaluating the ability to meet deadlines and deliverables.
- Smooth Functioning: Monitoring the seamless operation of organizational processes and systems.

Integrating the Four Cultures

Each of these cultural archetypes offers a different approach to managing an organization. In practice, most organizations exhibit elements of all four cultures but may prioritize one over the others depending on their strategic goals and operational needs. Understanding these cultural dimensions helps leaders create an environment that aligns with their organizational objectives and enhances overall effectiveness. Balancing the strengths of each cultural type can lead to a more adaptive, innovative, and performance-oriented organization

CHAPTER 4

STRATEGIC HR

Question

The first three chapters have provided us with a comprehensive foundation: we've explored how to get started with building our team, structuring it effectively, and driving the desired behaviors and outcomes. As we implement these strategies and gain clarity on our current operations, it is crucial to maintain a forward-looking perspective to ensure long-term success. This concept, known as "three-box thinking," emphasizes the importance of not only reflecting on past experiences (which, for a startup, might include the insights and lessons brought by its founders) but also focusing on the present while strategically planning for the future.

Three-Box Thinking and Its Relevance to HR Functions

Box 1: Learning from the Past The first box involves reflecting on past experiences to gain valuable insights. For a startup, this includes leveraging the founders' experiences, lessons learned from early challenges, and successes. This historical perspective helps in understanding what has worked well and what hasn't, offering a solid foundation for decision-making. In HR, this might involve analyzing previous hiring practices, employee feedback, and organizational culture development efforts to identify patterns and areas for improvement.

Box 2: Managing the Present The second box focuses on current operations and the immediate environment. For HR, this means implementing and optimizing the systems and structures we've developed. It involves managing day-to-day HR functions such as recruitment, onboarding, performance management, and employee engagement. Effective management of the present ensures that current processes are functioning efficiently and that the team is aligned with organizational goals. It also means adapting to immediate challenges and making necessary adjustments to meet current needs.

Box 3: Creating the Future The third box emphasizes the importance of strategic foresight and planning for the future. This involves anticipating changes, trends, and developments that may impact the organization. In HR, this could include strategic initiatives such as workforce planning, talent development, and cultivating a culture of innovation. It involves setting long-term goals and preparing the organization to adapt to evolving market conditions, technological advancements, and shifts in employee expectations.

Strategic HR and Future Planning

Strategic HR is a crucial component of Box 3, as it focuses on aligning human resources practices with the organization's long-term goals and vision. It involves proactive planning and strategic decision-making to ensure that the HR function supports the broader objectives of the organization. Key aspects of strategic HR include:

Workforce Planning: Develop a comprehensive plan for future workforce needs. This involves forecasting talent requirements based on organizational goals, industry trends, and potential growth opportunities. Effective workforce planning ensures that the organization has the right people in place to meet future demands.

Talent Development: Invest in programs that foster continuous learning and development. This includes creating career development pathways, offering training and development opportunities, and supporting employees in acquiring new skills. Talent development helps prepare employees for future roles and ensures that the organization has a capable and adaptable workforce.

Innovation and Change Management: Embrace innovation and prepare for change. This involves staying informed about emerging trends, technologies, and best practices in HR and incorporating them into the organization's strategy. Change management practices help facilitate smooth transitions and ensure that the organization remains agile and competitive.

Building a Resilient Culture: Cultivate a culture that supports adaptability, collaboration, and forward-thinking. A resilient culture is essential for navigating uncertainties and embracing new opportunities. This includes fostering an environment where employees are encouraged to contribute ideas, challenge the status quo, and engage in continuous improvement.

Long-Term Strategic Goals: Align HR strategies with the organization's long-term vision and strategic goals. This involves setting objectives that support the overall mission of the company and measuring progress against these goals. Strategic HR ensures that human resources initiatives are contributing to the achievement of the organization's broader objectives.

By integrating three-box thinking into your HR strategy, you can effectively balance past insights, current operations, and future planning. Strategic HR serves as a vital tool in shaping the future of the organization, ensuring that it remains adaptable, innovative, and aligned with its long-term goals. This holistic approach enables you to build a strong foundation while preparing for sustained success in an ever-changing environment.

Benefits of strategic planning

Strategic planning is a crucial process for guiding an organization towards its long-term goals and ensuring its overall success. Here's a detailed look at the benefits of strategic planning:

Avoid Costly and Disruptive Surprises

Strategic planning helps organizations anticipate potential challenges and uncertainties by providing a structured approach to identifying and analyzing risks. By proactively addressing these risks, organizations can avoid sudden, costly, and disruptive surprises that could derail progress toward their goals. This foresight allows businesses to develop contingency plans, allocate resources effectively, and implement preventive measures, ultimately reducing the likelihood of unexpected setbacks.

Address Key Issues Promptly to Avoid Crises

A well-crafted strategic plan ensures that key issues are identified and addressed in a timely manner. By continuously monitoring internal and external environments, organizations can detect emerging problems early and implement solutions before they escalate into crises. This proactive approach minimizes the impact of potential disruptions and maintains organizational stability, enabling the company to stay on course towards its objectives.

Promote Employee Productivity and Overall Organizational Success

Strategic planning aligns organizational objectives with individual roles and responsibilities, creating a clear pathway for employees to contribute effectively. When employees understand how their work supports the organization's goals, they are more motivated and productive. This alignment fosters a sense of purpose and enhances job satisfaction, which, in turn, drives overall organizational success by improving performance and achieving strategic targets.

Provide a Sense of Direction to Affect How Work Gets Done Positively

A strategic plan offers a clear sense of direction by outlining long-term goals and the steps required to achieve them. This clarity helps guide day-to-day operations and decision-making processes, ensuring that all activities are aligned with the organization's vision and mission. A well-defined direction enhances focus and coherence in efforts, leading to more effective and efficient execution of tasks and projects.

Keep Employees Focused on Organizational Goals

Strategic planning helps maintain employee focus on the organization's goals by setting clear priorities and performance expectations. Regular communication of the strategic plan and its objectives ensures that employees are aware of the organization's goals and how their individual contributions support them. This alignment fosters a unified effort towards achieving shared objectives and reinforces commitment to organizational success.

Provide a Strategic Focus to Guide Training and Development Initiatives

Strategic planning identifies the skills and competencies needed to achieve the organization's goals. This insight allows for the development of targeted training and development programs that address specific needs and gaps. By aligning training initiatives with strategic priorities, organizations can build a skilled workforce that is better equipped to execute the strategy and drive performance improvements.

Give Leaders Tools to Focus and Implement Strategic Initiatives

Leaders benefit from strategic planning by gaining access to tools and frameworks that facilitate the implementation of strategic initiatives. These tools include performance metrics, action plans, and monitoring systems that help leaders track progress, make informed decisions, and adjust strategies as needed. By providing a structured approach to strategy execution, leaders can effectively steer the organization towards its goals and ensure that strategic initiatives are successfully realized.

Strategic planning offers a multitude of benefits that contribute to the overall success and stability of an organization. It enables organizations to anticipate and mitigate risks, address issues proactively, enhance employee productivity, provide clear direction, maintain focus on goals, guide training efforts, and equip leaders with essential tools for implementation. By embracing strategic planning, organizations can better navigate the complexities of their operating environment and achieve long-term success.

Developing a strategic HR plan

Developing a strategic HR plan involves a structured approach that aligns human resource management with the overall strategic goals of the organization. This process typically begins with answering four critical questions that guide the development and implementation of the HR strategy. Here's a detailed breakdown of each question and its role in shaping a strategic HR plan:

Where Are We Now? (Assess the Current Situation)

Objective: The first step in developing a strategic HR plan is to evaluate the current state of the organization's human resources. This assessment provides a baseline understanding of where the organization stands in terms of HR capabilities, practices, and challenges.

Key Actions

- Conduct a Workforce Analysis: Evaluate the current composition of the workforce, including skills, competencies, and performance levels. Identify strengths, weaknesses, and gaps in skills.
- Review HR Practices: Analyze existing HR policies, procedures, and practices. Assess their effectiveness and alignment with organizational goals.
- Analyze HR Metrics: Examine key HR metrics such as employee turnover rates, absenteeism, and employee satisfaction. These metrics provide insights into the health and effectiveness of current HR practices.

- Engage Stakeholders: Gather feedback from employees, managers, and other stakeholders to understand their perspectives on HR practices and needs.

Where Do We Want to Be? (Envision and Articulate a Desired Future)

Objective: The second step involves defining the future state of the HR function and how it aligns with the organization's strategic objectives. This involves envisioning the desired outcomes and setting clear goals for the HR function.

Key Actions

Define HR Vision and Mission: Establish a clear vision and mission for the HR function that supports the overall organizational strategy. This provides direction and purpose for HR initiatives.

Set Strategic HR Goals: Identify specific, measurable, achievable, relevant, and time-bound (SMART) goals for the HR function. These goals should align with the organization's broader strategic objectives.

Envision HR Capabilities: Determine the future capabilities and competencies required to support the organization's strategic goals. This includes identifying new skills, technologies, and processes needed.

How Do We Get There? (Formulate and Implement a Strategy and Strategic Objectives)

Objective: This step involves developing a strategic plan that outlines how the HR function will achieve the desired future state. It includes formulating specific strategies, initiatives, and action plans.

Key Actions

- Develop HR Strategies: Create strategies that address the identified gaps and opportunities. This may include recruitment strategies, training and development programs, performance management systems, and employee engagement initiatives.

- Set Strategic Objectives: Establish clear objectives for each HR strategy. For example, if the strategy is to improve talent acquisition, objectives might include reducing time-to-fill positions and increasing the quality of hires.
- Create an Action Plan: Develop a detailed action plan outlining the steps, resources, and timelines required to implement each strategy. Assign responsibilities and allocate resources to ensure effective execution.
- Integrate with Organizational Strategy: Ensure that HR strategies and initiatives are closely aligned with the overall organizational strategy and support its long-term goals.

How Will We Know if We Are on Track Toward Our Intended Destination? (Establish a Mechanism to Evaluate Progress)

Objective: The final step involves setting up a system to monitor progress and evaluate the effectiveness of the HR strategies and initiatives. This ensures that the HR function stays on track and can make adjustments as needed.

Key Actions

- Define Key Performance Indicators (KPIs): Establish KPIs to measure progress toward strategic HR goals. Examples include employee retention rates, training effectiveness, and employee satisfaction scores.
- Implement Monitoring Systems: Use HR dashboards, performance management systems, and regular reports to track progress against the defined KPIs. Ensure that data collection and analysis are consistent and reliable.
- Conduct Regular Reviews: Schedule periodic reviews to assess progress, identify any issues, and make necessary adjustments

to strategies and action plans. This helps in staying aligned with organizational goals and adapting to changing circumstances.

- Solicit Feedback: Continuously gather feedback from employees and managers to gauge the impact of HR initiatives and identify areas for improvement.

Developing a strategic HR plan involves a systematic approach to assessing the current state, envisioning the desired future, formulating strategies, and evaluating progress. By answering the four critical questions—where are we now, where do we want to be, how do we get there, and how will we know if we are on track—organizations can create a comprehensive HR plan that supports their strategic objectives and drives overall success. This process ensures that HR practices are aligned with organizational goals, addresses key challenges, and fosters a productive and engaged workforce.

Develop strategic HR objectives

Developing strategic HR objectives is a critical component of aligning human resource management with the broader goals of the organization. To ensure these objectives are effective and actionable, they should address several key criteria. Here's how to evaluate and develop strategic HR objectives:

Have the Benefits of Obtaining the Defined Objectives Been Outlined and Communicated?

Objective: Clearly define and communicate the benefits of achieving the strategic HR objectives to ensure alignment and buy-in from all stakeholders.

Actions

Articulate Benefits: Identify and detail the specific benefits that achieving these objectives will bring to the organization. For example, improving employee engagement might lead to higher productivity and reduced turnover.

Communication Plan: Develop a communication strategy to share the benefits with employees, management, and other stakeholders. This can include presentations, written reports, and regular updates.

Feedback Mechanism: Implement a system for stakeholders to provide feedback on the objectives and their benefits, ensuring that any concerns or suggestions are addressed.

Are the Strategic Objectives Relevant to the Organization's Position in the External Market?

Objective: Ensure that the strategic HR objectives are aligned with the organization's external market conditions and competitive landscape.

Actions

Market Analysis: Conduct a thorough analysis of the external market, including competitor positions, market trends, and economic conditions. Assess how these factors impact the organization's strategic HR needs.

Relevance Check: Evaluate whether the strategic objectives are relevant given the organization's size, financial strength, and competitive position. For instance, if the organization is in a highly competitive industry, objectives might focus on attracting top talent.

Adaptation: Adjust the objectives as needed to reflect changes in the external environment and maintain their relevance.

Do the Strategic Objectives Recognize the Organization's Strengths and Weaknesses?

Objective: Develop objectives that leverage the organization's strengths and address its weaknesses.

Actions

SWOT Analysis: Perform a SWOT analysis (Strengths, Weaknesses, Opportunities, Threats) to identify internal strengths and weaknesses.

Objective Alignment: Ensure that the strategic objectives capitalize on strengths (e.g., leveraging a strong training program) and mitigate weaknesses (e.g., addressing skill gaps).

Continuous Assessment: Regularly review and update objectives to reflect changes in organizational strengths and weaknesses.

Do Employees Throughout the Company Understand How These Objectives Affect Them and How They Contribute Independently and Collectively to the Defined Objectives?

Objective: Ensure that all employees understand their role in achieving the strategic HR objectives and how their contributions impact the overall goals.

Actions

- Clear Communication: Communicate the strategic objectives clearly to all employees, explaining how their individual roles and responsibilities contribute to these goals.
- Training and Development: Provide training and development opportunities to help employees understand and align with the objectives.
- Involvement: Engage employees in the planning process and solicit their input to increase their commitment and understanding of the objectives.

Are the Strategic Objectives Realistic and Feasible?

Objective: Set objectives that are achievable and practical, avoiding unrealistic goals that can lead to disappointment and disengagement.

Actions

- Feasibility Assessment: Evaluate the resources, time, and capabilities required to achieve the objectives. Ensure they are realistic given the organization's current state and constraints.

- Benchmarking: Compare the objectives with industry standards and best practices to ensure they are achievable.
- Flexibility: Build in flexibility to adjust objectives as needed based on changing circumstances or unforeseen challenges.

Have Timelines for Benchmarking Progress and Targets for Completed Objectives Been Set?

Objective: Establish clear timelines and benchmarks to track progress and measure the achievement of strategic HR objectives.

Actions

- Timeline Development: Set specific deadlines for achieving each objective and interim milestones to track progress.
- Benchmarking: Define key performance indicators (KPIs) and benchmarks to measure progress towards the objectives.
- Review Schedule: Implement a regular review schedule to assess progress and make necessary adjustments.

Will the Organization Realistically Be Able to Identify the Success or Lack of Success in the Accomplishment of Strategic Objectives in Some Quantitative Fashion?

Objective: Ensure that success can be measured quantitatively to assess the effectiveness of the strategic HR objectives.

Actions

- Define Metrics: Identify quantitative metrics and KPIs that will be used to measure success. Examples might include turnover rates, employee satisfaction scores, or training completion rates.
- Data Collection: Implement systems for collecting and analyzing data related to the objectives.
- Performance Tracking: Regularly track and review performance data to evaluate the success of the objectives.

Can the Strategic Objectives Be Linked Back to the Organization's Overall Strategy?

Objective: Ensure that strategic HR objectives are aligned with and support the organization's overall strategy.

Actions:

- Strategic Alignment: Map HR objectives to the organization's broader strategic goals to ensure alignment and support.
- Integration: Integrate HR objectives into the overall strategic plan and ensure that they contribute to the achievement of organizational goals.
- Consistency: Regularly review the alignment of HR objectives with the organization's evolving strategy to maintain consistency.

Developing strategic HR objectives involves a comprehensive approach to ensure they are well-defined, relevant, and achievable. By addressing the outlined criteria—benefits, relevance, strengths and weaknesses, employee understanding, realism, timelines, measurability, and alignment with overall strategy—organizations can create effective HR objectives that support their strategic goals and drive success.

So, what do we do next?

Developing and executing a strategic HR plan involves several critical steps to ensure that objectives and action plans align with both organizational and HR strategies. Here's a detailed guide on how to effectively develop and implement strategic HR objectives:

Continuously Ensure That the Objective and Action Plan Are Aligned with the Organizational and HR Strategy

Objective: Maintain alignment between HR objectives, action plans, and the overall organizational strategy to ensure cohesive progress toward business goals.

Actions:

- Regular Review: Periodically review the alignment of HR objectives with the organization's strategic goals. This involves assessing whether the HR strategies support the broader business objectives and make necessary adjustments.
- Cross-functional Coordination: Engage with other departments and leadership teams to ensure that HR objectives are integrated with the organization's overall strategic plan.
- Strategic Alignment Check: Utilize tools such as balanced scorecards or strategy maps to visualize and verify the alignment of HR activities with organizational goals.

Identify the Primary Actions Required to Achieve the Objective

Objective: Determine the specific actions needed to reach the strategic HR objectives and develop a clear plan of action.

Actions:

- Action Plan Development: Break down the strategic objective into actionable steps. For example, if the objective is to improve employee engagement, actions might include conducting surveys, implementing feedback mechanisms, and developing employee recognition programs.
- Assign Responsibilities: Designate team members or departments responsible for each action. Ensure that roles and responsibilities are clearly defined.
- Action Sequencing: Prioritize actions based on their importance and logical sequence, ensuring that prerequisites are completed before subsequent steps are initiated.

Set Milestones for Each Action, and Plan for Contingencies

Objective: Establish milestones to track progress and prepare for potential challenges by developing contingency plans.

Actions:

- Milestone Definition: Set specific, measurable milestones for each action step. For instance, if implementing a new training program, milestones might include designing the curriculum, piloting the program, and full-scale implementation.
- Contingency Planning: Identify potential risks or obstacles that could impede progress. Develop contingency plans to address these risks, such as alternative resources or solutions.
- Progress Monitoring: Regularly review progress against milestones and adjust plans as necessary to stay on track.

Identify the Required Resources, Including Budget and Staff

Objective: Determine and allocate the necessary resources to support the execution of the strategic HR plan.

Actions:

- Resource Assessment: Identify the resources needed, including budget, personnel, technology, and materials. For example, if a new HR system is being implemented, resources may include software, hardware, and training for staff.
- Budget Planning: Develop a detailed budget that includes costs for each action step, such as salaries, training expenses, or technology investments.
- Staff Allocation: Assign appropriate staff or teams to carry out the actions, ensuring they have the necessary skills and capacity to achieve the objectives.

Establish Success Measures

Objective: Define how success will be measured to evaluate the effectiveness of the strategic HR objectives.

Actions:

- Success Metrics: Establish key performance indicators (KPIs) and success metrics relevant to each objective. For example, for improving employee retention, success measures might include turnover rates, employee satisfaction scores, and retention rates.
- Baseline Data: Gather baseline data to compare against future performance, enabling accurate measurement of progress and success.
- Evaluation Process: Develop a process for regularly assessing success measures, including setting review dates and defining evaluation criteria.

Communicate Key Messages

Objective: Ensure clear and effective communication of key messages related to the strategic HR objectives to all stakeholders.

Actions:

- Communication Plan: Create a communication plan outlining how and when key messages will be delivered. This can include updates through meetings, emails, or internal newsletters.
- Stakeholder Engagement: Identify key stakeholders and tailor messages to address their interests and concerns. Ensure that communication is transparent and provides relevant information.
- Feedback Mechanism: Implement a system for receiving feedback from stakeholders on the communicated messages. Use this feedback to refine communication strategies and address any issues or misunderstandings.

Effectively developing and implementing strategic HR objectives requires a systematic approach that includes ensuring alignment with organizational goals, identifying required actions, setting milestones, allocating resources, measuring success, and communicating key messages. By following these steps, HR professionals can create a robust plan that drives organizational success, aligns with strategic objectives, and effectively manages resources and risks.

How do we future-proof?

To ensure the effectiveness of the strategic HR plan and drive organizational success, the HR team must focus on several key areas and conduct periodic monitoring and evaluation. Here's a detailed breakdown of these responsibilities and the approach for ongoing assessment:

Key Responsibilities of the HR Team

Clarity of Communication

Objective: Ensure that all communication regarding HR strategies, objectives, and actions is clear, consistent, and effectively reaches all stakeholders.

Actions:

- Develop Clear Messaging: Craft clear and concise messages about HR objectives, strategies, and action plans. Use simple language and avoid jargon to ensure understanding across the organization.
- Utilize Multiple Channels: Employ various communication channels such as meetings, emails, newsletters, and intranet posts to disseminate information effectively.
- Regular Updates: Provide regular updates on progress, changes, and achievements to keep employees informed and engaged.

Alignment of Practices

Objective: Ensure that HR practices and policies are aligned with the strategic objectives of the organization.

Actions:

- Policy Review: Regularly review HR policies and practices to ensure they align with the strategic goals and objectives. Make adjustments as necessary to maintain alignment.
- Consistency: Ensure consistency in the application of HR practices across different departments and levels of the organization.
- Feedback Mechanism: Implement a feedback system to gather input from employees and managers on the effectiveness of HR practices and their alignment with strategic goals.

Leadership

Objective: Provide strong leadership to guide the HR function and support the organization in achieving its strategic objectives.

Actions:

- Strategic Leadership: Demonstrate leadership by actively participating in strategic planning and decision-making processes. Ensure HR leaders are involved in discussions on organizational strategy.
- Development Programs: Invest in leadership development programs to enhance the skills and capabilities of HR leaders and managers.
- Role Modeling: Model desired behaviors and practices, such as effective communication and strategic thinking, to inspire and guide the HR team.

An Adaptive Organizational Infrastructure

Objective: Develop and maintain an organizational infrastructure that is flexible and capable of adapting to changes.

Actions:

- Flexible Systems: Implement flexible HR systems and processes that can be adjusted in response to changes in the organizational environment or strategic direction.

- Change Management: Develop change management strategies to help the organization adapt to significant changes, including internal restructuring or external market shifts.
- Continuous Improvement: Foster a culture of continuous improvement by encouraging feedback and innovation within the HR function and the broader organization.

Resource Management

Objective: Ensure effective management of resources, including budget, personnel, and technology, to support the strategic HR plan.

Actions:

- Budget Management: Develop and manage a budget that supports HR initiatives and ensures efficient use of resources.
- Staff Allocation: Allocate personnel effectively to support HR objectives, ensuring that team members have the necessary skills and capacity.
- Technology Utilization: Invest in and utilize technology to streamline HR processes and improve efficiency.

Periodic Monitoring and Evaluation

Determine Whether the Organization is on Track to Achieve Key Objectives.

Objective: Regularly assess progress toward achieving strategic HR objectives and ensure the organization is on track.

Actions:

- Progress Reviews: Conduct regular reviews of progress against established objectives and milestones. Use performance metrics and KPIs to evaluate achievement levels.
- Reporting: Prepare and present progress reports to leadership and stakeholders, highlighting successes, challenges, and areas requiring attention.

- Adjustments: Make necessary adjustments to strategies and action plans based on progress reviews to ensure continued alignment with organizational goals.

Provide the Opportunity to Identify and Adapt to Significant Internal or External Changes That Affect the Strategic Plan

Objective: Monitor internal and external environments to identify changes that may impact the strategic HR plan and adapt accordingly.

Actions:

- Environmental Scanning: Regularly conduct environmental scans to identify significant changes, such as shifts in market conditions, regulatory changes, or internal organizational developments.
- Impact Assessment: Assess the impact of these changes on the strategic HR plan and determine the need for modifications or new strategies.
- Adaptation: Implement necessary changes to the HR plan in response to identified shifts to maintain relevance and effectiveness.

Update Annual Action Priorities

Objective: Review and update action priorities annually to reflect changes in the organizational strategy and external environment.

Actions:

- Annual Review: Conduct an annual review of the strategic HR plan to evaluate the relevance and effectiveness of current priorities.
- Reprioritization: Adjust action priorities based on the review findings, including new objectives, emerging needs, or changes in organizational strategy.

- Communication: Communicate updated priorities to all stakeholders and ensure that action plans are revised and aligned with the new priorities.

To effectively implement and manage a strategic HR plan, the HR team must ensure clarity of communication, alignment of practices, strong leadership, adaptive infrastructure, and efficient resource management. Periodic monitoring and evaluation are crucial for assessing progress, adapting to changes, and updating priorities. By focusing on these areas, the HR team can drive organizational success and support the achievement of strategic goals

The case of Industry 4.0

As Industry 4.0 revolutionizes the manufacturing landscape with technologies like driverless cars, self-driving forklifts, and smart machines, HR must evolve strategically to address the profound changes and leverage opportunities presented by these advancements. Here's how HR can build a strategic HR plan in the context of Industry 4.0:

Understanding the Strategic HR Plan in the Context of Industry 4.0

Align HR Strategy with Industry 4.0 Objectives

Objective: Ensure that the HR strategy aligns with the broader organizational goals related to Industry 4.0, such as adopting new technologies and improving efficiency.

Actions:

- Strategic Alignment: Collaborate with leadership to understand the organization's Industry 4.0 goals and integrate these into the HR strategy. For instance, if the goal is to enhance automation, HR should focus on skills development related to robotics and AI.

- Technology Integration: Align HR practices with new technologies. This could involve incorporating AI for talent acquisition and big data for performance management.

Develop Skills and Capabilities for Industry 4.0

Objective: Equip employees with the necessary skills to operate and thrive in a technology-driven environment.

Actions:

- Skills Assessment: Conduct a comprehensive skills assessment to identify gaps between current employee skills and those required for Industry 4.0 technologies. This includes knowledge of cyber-physical systems, IoT, robotics, and data analysis.
- Training Programs: Develop and implement targeted training programs to address skill gaps. This might include upskilling in areas such as robotics maintenance, data analytics, and software programming.
- Continuous Learning: Foster a culture of continuous learning and adaptability. Encourage employees to pursue further education and certifications relevant to Industry 4.0 technologies.

Adapt Recruitment and Talent Management

Objective: Attract, recruit, and retain talent with the skills necessary for Industry 4.0.

Actions:

- Talent Acquisition: Revise recruitment strategies to attract candidates with expertise in emerging technologies. Use advanced tools such as AI-driven recruitment platforms to streamline the hiring process.
- Talent Pools: Build and maintain talent pools with skills in high demand, such as AI specialists, data scientists, and robotics engineers.

- Retention Strategies: Develop retention strategies that include career development opportunities and competitive compensation packages to keep valuable talent.

Design and Implement Adaptive Organizational Structures

Objective: Create an organizational structure that supports flexibility and responsiveness in a rapidly changing technological environment.

Actions:

- Organizational Design: Redesign organizational structures to support cross-functional collaboration and innovation. For instance, establish teams that focus on specific Industry 4.0 technologies and encourage interdepartmental cooperation.
- Agility: Implement agile methodologies in project management to enable rapid adaptation to technological changes and market demands.

Invest in Technology and Infrastructure

Objective: Ensure that the organization's HR function is equipped to handle the technological demands of Industry 4.0.

Actions:

HR Technology: Invest in advanced HR technologies, such as cloud-based HR systems, AI-driven analytics for talent management, and virtual reality for employee training and onboarding.

Infrastructure Upgrades: Ensure that the necessary technological infrastructure is in place to support the new technologies and processes introduced by Industry 4.0.

Foster a Culture of Innovation and Change

Objective: Cultivate a workplace culture that embraces change and innovation, which is critical for adapting to Industry 4.0.

Actions:

- Change Management: Implement change management practices to help employees adapt to new technologies and processes. This includes clear communication, training, and support systems.
- Innovation Encouragement: Encourage a culture of innovation by rewarding creative problem-solving and experimentation. Provide platforms for employees to contribute ideas and engage in innovation.

Monitor and Evaluate HR Strategies and Initiatives

Objective: Regularly assess the effectiveness of HR strategies and initiatives in the context of Industry 4.0.

Actions:

- Performance Metrics: Establish metrics to evaluate the success of HR initiatives related to Industry 4.0. This might include measuring the impact of training programs, recruitment effectiveness, and employee engagement.
- Feedback Mechanisms: Implement feedback mechanisms to gather input from employees on the effectiveness of HR strategies and initiatives. Use this feedback to make continuous improvements.
- Regular Reviews: Conduct periodic reviews of HR strategies to ensure they remain aligned with evolving Industry 4.0 objectives and technological advancements.

Building a strategic HR plan in the context of Industry 4.0 involves aligning HR strategies with organizational goals, developing skills and capabilities, adapting recruitment and talent management, designing adaptive organizational structures, investing in technology, fostering a culture of innovation, and continuously monitoring and evaluating HR initiatives. By focusing on these areas, HR can effectively support the organization's transition into the fourth industrial revolution and ensure it remains competitive in an increasingly technology-driven landscape.

The future challenge: Industry 4.0	Impact on HR Practices	HR Success Factors	Successful strategic HR plan
	Job Design	Restructuring of jobs	
	Recruitment	Attracting qualified and smart employees to dominate sophisticated and complex technologies of Industry 4.0	
	Training	Retraining and upskilling of employees	
	Development	Appropriate development programs	
	Compensation	Competitive compensation	
	Impact on HR Practices	HR Success Factors	
	Performance Appraisal	Performance appraisal system focused on the employee development	
	Safety and work conditions	Adequate and right-working conditions	
		Smart HRM practices	

Table 1: Strategic HR plan for Industry 4.0

CHAPTER 5

ROLE OF HRBP

Question

The role of an HR Business Partner (HRBP) is multifaceted and critical to aligning human resources with organizational strategy. This book aims to provide a comprehensive HRBP Toolkit, outlining the essential processes and activities HRBPs must engage in to fulfil their role effectively. Below is a detailed list of key processes and activities that an HRBP should perform, organized into a toolkit format:

HRBP Toolkit: Essential Processes and Activities

Strategic Alignment

- Business Strategy Integration:

  - Collaborate with senior management to understand business goals and strategies.
  - Ensure HR initiatives and policies align with the organization's strategic objectives.

- Strategic Planning:

  - Contribute to the development of long-term HR strategies that support business growth.
  - Participate in strategic meetings and provide HR insights to influence business decisions.

Talent Management

- Workforce Planning:

  - Analyze current workforce capabilities and forecast future talent needs.
  - Develop strategies to address talent gaps and manage succession planning.

- Talent Acquisition:

  - Partner with recruitment teams to design effective job descriptions and candidate profiles.
  - Support the recruitment process by participating in interviews and selecting candidates.

- Employee Development:

  - Identify training and development needs in alignment with business goals.
  - Design and implement development programs to enhance employee skills and leadership capabilities.

Performance Management

- Goal Setting:

  - Assist in setting performance objectives that align with business priorities.
  - Ensure that performance goals are clear, measurable, and achievable.

- Performance Reviews:

  - Facilitate the performance evaluation process, including feedback and appraisal discussions.
  - Provide support to managers in addressing performance issues and setting improvement plans.

Organizational Development

- Change Management:

  - Develop and execute change management strategies to support organizational transitions.
  - Communicate effectively with employees about changes and manage their impact.

- Culture and Engagement:

  - Promote and reinforce organizational culture and values.
  - Implement initiatives to enhance employee engagement and satisfaction.

Employee Relations

- Conflict Resolution:

  - Address employee grievances and resolve conflicts in a fair and timely manner.
  - Mediate disputes and provide solutions that support a positive work environment.

- Employee Support:

  - Offer guidance on HR-related matters such as career development, compensation, and benefits.
  - Act as a liaison between employees and management to address concerns and provide support.

Compliance and Risk Management

- Policy Adherence:

  - Ensure HR practices comply with legal regulations and company policies.
  - Stay informed about changes in labor laws and industry standards.

- Risk Management:

  - Identify and manage HR-related risks, including workplace safety and employee misconduct.
  - Develop strategies to mitigate legal and operational risks.

Data-Driven Decision Making

- HR Analytics:

  - Use data and analytics to inform HR strategies and decisions.
  - Monitor key metrics such as employee turnover, performance trends, and engagement levels.

- Reporting:

  - Prepare and present reports on HR metrics and the impact of HR initiatives.
  - Provide insights and recommendations based on data analysis.

Employee Advocacy

- Voice of Employees:

  - Represent employee interests in discussions with management.
  - Advocate for policies and practices that support employee needs and well-being.

- Wellbeing Initiatives:

  - Develop and implement programs to promote employee health and work-life balance.
  - Support initiatives that enhance overall employee satisfaction and productivity.

Communication and Collaboration

- Stakeholder Communication:

    o Maintain open lines of communication with business leaders, employees, and other stakeholders.

    o Ensure that HR messages and initiatives are effectively communicated throughout the organization.

- Cross-Functional Collaboration:

    o Work closely with other departments to support organizational objectives.

    o Collaborate on projects and initiatives that require HR input and expertise.

The HRBP Toolkit provides a structured approach to the diverse responsibilities of an HR Business Partner. By focusing on strategic alignment, talent management, performance management, organizational development, employee relations, compliance, data-driven decision making, employee advocacy, and communication, HRBPs can effectively contribute to the success of their organization. This toolkit serves as a practical guide for HRBPs to navigate their role and make a meaningful impact on both human resources and business outcomes.

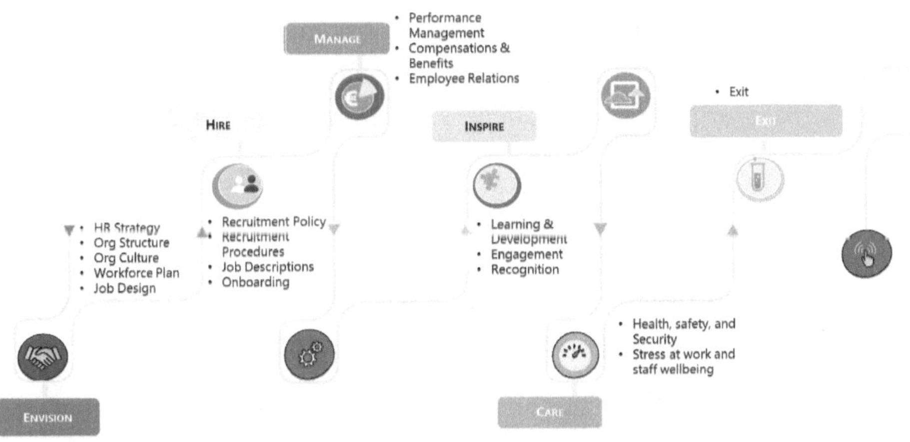

Figure 6: HR Business Partner Role Took-Kit

Envision

HR Strategy

Developing an Effective HR Strategy

An effective HR strategy is essential for aligning and integrating culture, people, and systems with organizational goals and vision. It requires coordination, support from leadership, and a focus on best practices. Here's a breakdown of key considerations for developing and implementing a robust HR strategy:

Valuing and Recognizing Staff Contributions

Objective: Ensure that the organizational strategy explicitly acknowledges and values the contributions of staff toward achieving organizational objectives.

Considerations:

- Recognition Programs: Implement formal recognition programs to celebrate employee achievements and contributions. This could include awards, bonuses, or public acknowledgments.
- Performance Appraisals: Develop a performance appraisal system that provides constructive feedback and highlights how individual contributions align with organizational goals.
- Communication: Clearly communicate how staff contributions impact organizational success. Regularly update employees on how their work supports the broader objectives.

Key Questions:

- Does your organizational strategy explicitly value and recognize staff for their contributions to organizational objectives?
  - Ensure that recognition and reward systems are embedded in the organizational strategy and are communicated effectively to all employees.

Implementing Contributions and Feedback

Objective: Actively implement and act upon contributions and feedback from staff to foster a responsive and inclusive work environment.

Considerations:

- Feedback Mechanisms: Establish channels for employees to provide feedback, such as surveys, suggestion boxes, or regular one-on-one meetings.
- Action Plans: Develop and implement action plans based on employee feedback to address concerns and improve processes.
- Transparency: Communicate the steps taken in response to feedback and contributions, and demonstrate how these actions align with organizational goals.

Key Questions:

- Does your organization follow through with implementing contributions and feedback from staff?

  - Evaluate how well the organization acts on feedback and integrates employee contributions into decision-making processes.

Allocating Resources to Achieve HR Strategy

Objective: Ensure that the organization allocates sufficient human and financial resources to effectively implement the HR strategy.

Considerations:

- Budget Allocation: Allocate a budget specifically for HR initiatives, including recruitment, training, development, and employee engagement.
- Resource Planning: Plan and allocate human resources effectively to support HR functions. This may involve hiring additional staff or providing training for existing employees.

- Resource Monitoring: Regularly review and adjust resource allocations based on the evolving needs of the HR strategy and organizational objectives.

Key Questions:

- Does your organizational strategy allocate sufficient human and financial resources to achieve its HR strategy?

  - Assess whether the resource allocation is adequate and aligned with the strategic HR goals and whether adjustments are made as needed.

Supporting Organizational Objectives and Commitments

Objective: Ensure that the HR strategy supports the organization's objectives and demonstrates a commitment to inclusiveness, diversity, and ethical standards.

Considerations:

- Inclusiveness and Diversity: Develop and implement policies and practices that promote a diverse and inclusive workplace. This includes recruitment, training, and career development initiatives.
- Ethical Standards: Establish clear policies to prohibit sexual exploitation and abuse, and ensure these policies are integrated into HR practices.
- Strategic Alignment: Regularly review the HR strategy to ensure it supports the overall organizational objectives and ethical commitments.

Key Questions:

- Does your HR strategy reflect and support your organization's objectives and commitment to promoting inclusiveness and diversity, and to prohibiting sexual exploitation and abuse?

    ○   Evaluate how well the HR strategy aligns with and supports the organization's commitment to diversity, inclusiveness, and ethical practices.

Developing an effective HR strategy involves aligning staff recognition with organizational goals, actively implementing feedback, allocating appropriate resources, and supporting organizational commitments to inclusiveness and ethical standards. By addressing these key areas, HR can effectively contribute to achieving organizational objectives and fostering a positive, inclusive, and ethical work environment.

Organizational Structure

Evaluating Organizational Structure

An effective organizational structure is crucial for defining job roles, functions, and reporting relationships within an organization. It helps in streamlining operations and ensuring clarity in management and communication. Here's how to evaluate the effectiveness and relevance of your organizational structure:

Accessibility of the Organizational Chart

Objective: Ensure that the organizational chart is readily accessible to all staff members so they can reference it as needed.

Considerations:

- Availability: Make the organizational chart available through easily accessible channels, such as the company intranet, employee handbook, or internal communication platforms.
- Visibility: Ensure that all employees are aware of where to find the chart and understand how to use it effectively.
- Regular Reminders: Periodically remind staff of the chart's availability, especially during onboarding processes or organizational changes.

Key Questions:

- Is the organizational chart available and easily accessible to all staff so they can reference it as required?

    o   Verify that the chart is placed in a central location where employees can easily access it whenever needed.

Accuracy and Currency of the Organizational Chart

Objective: Ensure that the organizational chart is accurate, up-to-date, and reflects the current structure of the organization.

Considerations:

- Update Schedule: Establish a regular schedule for reviewing and updating the organizational chart. This could be quarterly, biannually, or following major organizational changes.
- Change Tracking: Implement a process for updating the chart when there are changes in roles, reporting lines, or organizational structure. Designate responsibility for maintaining and updating the chart.
- Accuracy Checks: Conduct periodic audits to verify that the organizational chart accurately reflects the current structure and reporting lines.

Key Questions:

- Is the organizational chart accurate and up to date? When was it last updated? What is the process to update it?

    o   Determine the last update date and review the process for making changes to ensure it is effective and responsive to organizational needs.

Suitability of the Organizational Structure

Objective: Assess whether the current organizational structure supports the implementation of the organization's strategy and helps meet its goals.

Considerations:

- Alignment with Strategy: Evaluate whether the structure supports the strategic goals of the organization. For example, if the strategy involves rapid innovation, the structure should facilitate agile decision-making and cross-functional collaboration.
- Role Clarity: Ensure that the structure clearly defines roles and responsibilities in a way that supports organizational goals and objectives.
- Flexibility: Assess whether the structure is flexible enough to adapt to changes in strategy or business environment.

Key Questions:

- Is the structure (still) suitable to enable the implementation of the organization's strategy and meet its goals?

  - Analyze whether the current structure facilitates the execution of strategic initiatives and aligns with the organization's long-term objectives.

Clarity of Management and Communication Reporting Lines

Objective: Ensure that the organizational structure clearly outlines management and communication reporting lines.

Considerations:

- Reporting Lines: Verify that the chart clearly shows reporting relationships, including who reports to whom and how information flows within the organization.

- Communication Channels: Ensure that communication lines are clearly defined, promoting effective and efficient information exchange across the organization.
- Conflict Resolution: Establish clear lines for addressing and resolving issues related to reporting and communication.

Key Questions:

- Does the structure clearly explain the management and communication reporting lines?
  - Check if the organizational chart provides a clear depiction of management hierarchies and communication pathways.

To maintain an effective organizational structure, ensure that the organizational chart is easily accessible and regularly updated, accurately reflecting the current organizational hierarchy. Evaluate whether the structure supports the organization's strategic goals and provides clear management and communication reporting lines. Regularly review and adjust the structure as needed to align with strategic objectives and operational needs.

Organizational Culture

Evaluating Organizational Culture and HR Alignment

Organizational culture—the set of values, beliefs, norms, and habitual practices—profoundly influences HR management and overall organizational effectiveness. For HR to support and enhance this culture, it must ensure alignment between culture and people management practices. Here's how to assess this alignment and address related concerns:

Understanding and Aligning Organizational Culture

Objective: Assess how employees perceive the organization's culture and determine how well it supports the organization's goals.

Considerations:

- Employee Perception: Gather feedback from employees through surveys, interviews, or focus groups to understand their perspective on the organizational culture.
- Cultural Fit: Evaluate whether the current culture aligns with and supports the organization's strategic objectives and mission.
- Cultural Impact: Determine how the organizational culture influences employee behavior, satisfaction, and performance.

Key Questions:

- How would employees describe the culture of your organization? How well is the culture serving what the organization is trying to achieve?

  - Analyze employee feedback to gauge the perceived culture and its alignment with organizational goals. Identify any gaps and areas for improvement.

Evaluating People Management Practices

Objective: Ensure that people management practices are aligned with and support the desired cultural attributes of the organization.

Considerations:

- Performance Management: Assess whether the performance management system encourages and reinforces cultural values. For instance, does it recognize and reward behaviors that align with the organizational culture?
- Recognition and Rewards: Evaluate how recognition and reward systems reflect cultural values. Are they designed to promote desired behaviors and reinforce the culture?
- Learning and Development: Review access to learning and development opportunities. Ensure that these opportunities are

distributed equitably and support the cultural attributes of the organization.

Key Questions:

- Do people management interventions support and promote desired cultural attributes or conflict with them (e.g., how performance is managed, what is recognized and rewarded, who has access to learning and development opportunities)?

  - Assess whether HR practices reinforce or undermine the organizational culture. Make adjustments as needed to align practices with cultural values.

Code of Conduct and Ethical Standards

Objective: Ensure that a code of conduct is in place and that ethical standards and values are communicated and upheld.

Considerations:

- Code of Conduct: Implement a clear code of conduct that outlines expected behaviors and organizational values.
- Communication: Ensure that the code of conduct and ethical standards are effectively communicated to all staff members.
- Reporting Mechanisms: Provide multiple channels for employees to report breaches of the code of conduct or ethical issues, such as anonymous hotlines or designated HR contacts.

Key Questions:

- Do you have a code of conduct in place? Are the expected standards of behaviors and organizational values clearly communicated to staff? Do you have different channels to enable reporting of abuse and breaches of these?

  - Verify the existence and effectiveness of the code of conduct and reporting channels. Ensure that all employees are aware of and understand the code and how to report concerns.

Commitment to Equality, Diversity, and Inclusion (EDI)

Objective: Embed commitment to equality, diversity, and inclusion (EDI) within HR policies and practices.

Considerations:

- Policy Integration: Ensure that EDI principles are integrated into HR policies, including recruitment, training, and performance management.
- Practice Implementation: Review HR practices to ensure they promote and support diversity and inclusion. This might include equitable hiring practices, diversity training programs, and inclusive leadership development.
- Monitoring and Evaluation: Implement mechanisms for monitoring and evaluating the effectiveness of EDI policies and practices. Collect and analyze data to track progress and identify areas for improvement.
- *Key Questions:*
- How is your commitment to equality, diversity, and inclusion embedded in your HR policies and practices?
- Assess whether EDI principles are effectively integrated into HR policies and everyday practices. Review policies, training programs, and diversity metrics to ensure alignment with EDI commitments.

To effectively align organizational culture with HR practices, it's crucial to understand and support the prevailing culture through thoughtful management interventions, clear ethical standards, and a strong commitment to equality, diversity, and inclusion. Regularly evaluate employee perceptions, ensure HR practices reinforce cultural values, maintain clear codes of conduct, and integrate EDI principles into HR policies. By doing so, HR can foster a work environment that supports organizational goals and enables staff to thrive.

Workforce Planning

Workforce Planning: Key Components and Processes

Workforce planning is a strategic process designed to ensure that an organization has the right people in the right roles at the right time to meet its current and future needs. Effective workforce planning involves several critical components:

Determining Human Resource Needs

Objective: Assess the current and future human resource needs of the organization to align with its strategic goals and operational requirements.

Considerations:

- Current Workforce Analysis: Evaluate the current workforce to understand existing skills, competencies, and gaps.
- Future Needs Assessment: Project future human resource needs based on organizational growth, strategic objectives, market trends, and potential challenges.
- Skill Requirements: Identify the types of skills, knowledge, and experience required to meet both short-term and long-term goals.

Key Questions:

- What are the current and future human resource needs of the organization?
  - Determine the number of employees required, the types of skills needed, and the timeline for meeting these needs.

Creating the Correct Number and Type of Jobs

Objective: Design and structure the right number and types of jobs to fulfill the identified human resource needs effectively.

Considerations:

- Job Design: Develop job descriptions and specifications that clearly outline the roles, responsibilities, and qualifications needed for each position.
- Organizational Structure: Ensure that the organizational structure supports the creation of jobs that align with strategic goals and operational requirements.
- Role Clarity: Define roles and responsibilities to avoid overlaps and gaps, ensuring efficiency and effectiveness in job functions.

Key Questions:

- Does the organization have the correct number and type of jobs to meet its human resource needs?
  - Assess whether the job roles and organizational structure are aligned with the identified needs and strategic objectives.

Supporting Scale-Up of Human Resource Capacity

Objective: Prepare to scale human resource capacity quickly and effectively during periods of increased demand or organizational expansion.

Considerations:

- Flexibility and Scalability: Develop strategies to increase workforce capacity in response to business surges, including temporary hires, contract workers, or flexible work arrangements.
- Resource Allocation: Ensure that resources are allocated efficiently to support scaling efforts, including budget, training, and recruitment processes.
- Contingency Planning: Implement contingency plans to address unexpected changes in workforce needs or surges in demand.

Key Questions:

- How will the organization scale up its human resource capacity during times of surge?

    ○ Evaluate the strategies and resources in place for rapidly increasing workforce capacity as needed.

Recruiting the Right Skills, Knowledge, and Attitudes

Objective: Attract and hire individuals with the appropriate skills, knowledge, and attitudes to meet organizational needs and contribute to its success.

Considerations:

- Recruitment Strategy: Develop a recruitment strategy that targets candidates with the desired skills and competencies.
- Selection Process: Implement a rigorous selection process to ensure that candidates not only possess the necessary skills but also align with the organization's culture and values.
- Onboarding: Provide effective onboarding programs to integrate new hires smoothly and ensure they are well-prepared for their roles.

Key Questions:

- Is the organization recruiting individuals with the right skills, knowledge, and attitudes?

    ○ Assess the effectiveness of recruitment and selection processes in identifying and hiring suitable candidates.

Developing Existing Staff

Objective: Invest in the development of existing staff to enhance their skills and capabilities, ensuring the organization can achieve its current and future objectives.

Considerations:

- Training and Development: Implement training programs to address skill gaps and prepare employees for future roles and responsibilities.
- Career Pathing: Create clear career paths and development opportunities to retain talent and foster employee growth.
- Performance Management: Use performance management systems to identify development needs and track progress.

Key Questions:

- How does the organization develop existing staff to achieve both current objectives and long-term strategic goals?

  - Review training and development initiatives to ensure they support the organization's goals and employee career growth.

Effective workforce planning involves determining the human resource needs of the organization, creating appropriate job roles, scaling workforce capacity during surges, recruiting the right talent, and developing existing staff. By addressing these components, organizations can align their workforce with strategic objectives, support operational efficiency, and foster a capable and motivated team. Regular assessment and adjustment of workforce planning processes are essential to adapt to changing needs and ensure ongoing success.

Job Design

Evaluating Job Design Processes

Job design is a crucial process that involves creating or updating roles to ensure they align with organizational goals and effectively support program objectives. A well-designed job ensures that roles are clear, manageable, and aligned with the strategic needs of the organization. Here's how to evaluate and enhance your job design process:

Identification and Design of Existing Roles

Objective: Determine how roles are identified, designed, and whether there is a consistent approach to job design within the organization.

Considerations:

- Role Identification: Assess how new roles are identified and existing roles are updated. This may involve analyzing current job functions, gathering feedback from employees and managers, and reviewing organizational needs.
- Design Approach: Check if there is a standardized approach or framework for job design that ensures consistency and alignment with organizational objectives.
- Stakeholder Involvement: Ensure that key stakeholders, including managers, employees, and HR, are involved in the job design process to capture diverse perspectives and needs.

Key Questions:

- How are existing roles identified and designed? Is there a consistent approach to job design?

  - Evaluate the methods used for identifying and designing roles. Determine if there is a uniform approach or if practices vary across departments.

Recent Analysis and Review of Existing Roles

Objective: Ensure that existing roles are regularly analyzed and reviewed to remain relevant and effective.

Considerations:

- Review Frequency: Determine how often roles are reviewed and updated to reflect changes in organizational goals, technology, or workflows.

- Feedback Mechanisms: Implement mechanisms for ongoing feedback from employees and managers to identify necessary updates or improvements in job roles.
- Adaptation to Change: Ensure that the review process allows for adjustments in response to evolving business needs or external factors.

Key Questions:

- Have existing roles been analyzed/reviewed recently?
  - Check the timeline of the last review or update of job roles and assess whether the roles have been modified to keep pace with organizational changes.

Consideration of Specific Ways of Working

Objective: Assess whether the job design process takes into account various ways of working, such as matrix team management, project-based workflows, or remote management.

Considerations:

- Flexible Work Arrangements: Ensure that job designs accommodate different work arrangements and structures, including remote work, project-based teams, and matrix management.
- Workflow Integration: Evaluate how well job roles integrate with specific work processes and team structures to support efficiency and collaboration.
- Role Adaptability: Design roles to be adaptable to various working styles and organizational structures.

Key Questions:

- Does the job design process consider specific ways of working (i.e., matrix team management, project-based workflow, remote management, etc.)?

- ○ Review whether job roles are designed to support different organizational structures and working methods, and adjust designs as necessary.

Realistic Management Roles and Spans of Control

Objective: Ensure that management roles are designed with realistic spans of control, making them feasible and effective.

Considerations:

- Span of Control: Evaluate whether managers have a manageable number of direct reports. Excessive spans of control can lead to ineffective management and decreased employee engagement.
- Role Clarity: Ensure that managerial roles are clearly defined with appropriate authority, responsibilities, and resources to manage their teams effectively.
- Support Structures: Provide support mechanisms, such as assistant managers or team leads, to help manage larger teams if necessary.

Key Questions:

- Are management roles "doable" – designed with realistic spans of control?
  - ○ Assess whether the span of control for managers is practical and allows them to effectively oversee their teams.

Consistency in Job Evaluations and Grading

Objective: Ensure that job evaluations and grading are performed consistently across all categories of staff.

Considerations:

- Evaluation Criteria: Implement consistent criteria and processes for evaluating and grading jobs to ensure fairness and transparency.

- Grading Systems: Use a standardized grading system to categorize roles based on responsibilities, skills required, and other relevant factors.
- Periodic Reviews: Conduct regular reviews of job evaluations and grading practices to ensure they remain fair and aligned with industry standards.

Key Questions:

- Are the job evaluations and grading done consistently for all categories of staff?

  - Review the processes and criteria used for job evaluations and grading to ensure consistency and fairness across the organization.

Effective job design involves systematically identifying, designing, and reviewing roles to align with organizational goals and accommodate various working styles. Ensure that the job design process is consistent, considers specific ways of working, provides realistic management roles, and applies fair and consistent job evaluations and grading. Regularly review and update job roles to keep pace with organizational changes and maintain effectiveness.

Hire

Recruitment Policy

A recruitment policy serves as a foundational document that outlines an organization's approach to hiring, reflecting its values and principles while ensuring a consistent and fair process across all levels. To ensure that the recruitment policy is effective and meets organizational needs, especially in an international context, it is essential to address several key considerations. Here's a detailed examination of these considerations:

Contextualization for International Operations

Country-Specific Adaptation

Local Regulations and Practices: When operating internationally, it's crucial to adapt the recruitment policy to fit the legal, cultural, and economic contexts of each country. This involves understanding and complying with local labor laws, employment practices, and cultural norms.

Localized Recruitment Strategies: Tailor recruitment approaches to align with local job markets and talent pools. This may include adjusting job advertisements, recruitment channels, and selection criteria to better suit regional characteristics and expectations.

Consistency and Integration

Global Standards with Local Flexibility: While the overarching principles of the recruitment policy should remain consistent across all locations, there should be flexibility to accommodate local variations. This balance helps maintain organizational coherence while respecting regional differences.

Clarity of Responsibilities and Accountabilities

Defined Roles and Responsibilities

Clear Guidelines: Ensure that roles and responsibilities related to recruitment are clearly defined and communicated to all staff. This includes specifying who is responsible for various stages of the recruitment process, such as job posting, interviewing, and decision-making.

Accountability Mechanisms: Implement mechanisms to hold individuals accountable for their recruitment duties. This includes setting up clear procedures for reporting and addressing any deviations from the policy.

Communication

Policy Awareness: Ensure that all relevant staff are aware of the recruitment policy and their respective roles in the process. Regular training and updates can help reinforce understanding and adherence.

Diversity and Equality Policy

Inclusion Beyond Legal Requirements

Proactive Approach: Even if not mandated by law, having a diversity and equality policy demonstrates a commitment to creating an inclusive and equitable workplace. This policy should outline the organization's stance on promoting diversity, preventing discrimination, and ensuring equal opportunities for all candidates.

Integration into Recruitment: Incorporate diversity and equality principles into all aspects of the recruitment process, from job descriptions to selection criteria, to foster an inclusive hiring practice.

Training for Recruitment and Selection

Critical Skills Development

Interviewing Skills: Provide training to those involved in recruitment on effective interviewing techniques. This includes preparing questions that align with job requirements and assessing candidates objectively.

Diversity and Equality Training: Ensure that recruiters and hiring managers are trained on diversity and equality policies to prevent bias and ensure fair treatment of all candidates.

Ongoing Development

Continuous Learning: Offer ongoing training opportunities to keep staff updated on best practices and changes in recruitment standards. This includes workshops, seminars, and online courses.

Policy Appropriateness and Adaptation

Alignment with Organizational Needs

Relevance to Programs: Ensure that the recruitment policy is designed to meet the specific needs of different programs or departments within the organization. This involves understanding the unique requirements and skill sets needed for various roles.

Market Adaptation

Responsive to Market Trends: Adapt the policy to reflect changes in the job market, such as shifts in demand for certain skills or emerging recruitment trends. This helps in attracting and retaining the best talent.

Key Performance Indicators (KPIs)

Measuring Effectiveness

Relevant KPIs: Identify and track KPIs that reflect the effectiveness of the recruitment policy and practices. Common KPIs include time-to-fill, cost-per-hire, quality-of-hire, and candidate satisfaction.

Continuous Improvement: Use KPI data to assess and improve recruitment processes. Regularly review performance metrics to identify areas for enhancement and adjust policies accordingly.

Feedback Mechanisms

Soliciting Input: Gather feedback from candidates and hiring managers to understand their experiences with the recruitment process. This feedback can provide valuable insights into areas for improvement.

A well-crafted recruitment policy is essential for ensuring a fair, consistent, and effective hiring process. By contextualizing the policy for international operations, clarifying responsibilities, implementing a diversity and equality framework, providing adequate training, adapting to market needs, and measuring performance through KPIs, organizations can enhance their recruitment practices and better align them with their strategic goals. This comprehensive approach not only supports successful talent acquisition but also contributes to a positive and inclusive organizational culture.

Recruitment Procedures

Recruitment procedures are essential for guiding the process of attracting, selecting, and hiring the right candidates for an organization. Well-defined and properly executed recruitment practices ensure that the organization can build a diverse and skilled workforce, while also mitigating risks associated with hiring. Below is a detailed exploration of how to address various aspects of the recruitment process to ensure it is fair, transparent, and effective:

Mitigating Organizational Risks

Conduct Comprehensive Checks

Employment References: Verify previous employment details and obtain feedback from former employers to confirm the candidate's work history and performance.

Health Checks: Where applicable, ensure that candidates meet any health requirements for the role, while adhering to legal and ethical standards.

Criminal Records: Conduct background checks to uncover any potential issues that could pose risks to the organization. Ensure compliance with legal requirements and obtain candidate consent before conducting these checks.

Risk Assessment

Evaluate Risks: Identify potential risks associated with the recruitment process, such as biased decision-making or inadequate candidate vetting. Develop strategies to mitigate these risks and ensure compliance with relevant regulations.

Recruitment Documentation

Standardized Documentation

Consistency: Ensure that recruitment documentation, including job descriptions, interview notes, and selection criteria, is standardized and consistent across all positions.

Secure Storage: Store recruitment documents in a secure location with restricted access to protect candidate confidentiality and data integrity. Utilize secure digital storage solutions and maintain data protection compliance.

Feedback for Interviewed Candidates

Providing Feedback

Timely Communication: Offer constructive feedback to candidates who were interviewed but not selected. This can be done via email or phone and should include specific reasons for their non-selection.

Positive Experience: Providing feedback not only helps candidates improve but also maintains a positive image of the organization and can enhance future candidate engagement.

Encouraging Adherence to Recruitment Procedures

Clear Responsibilities

Role Definitions: Clearly define and communicate the roles and responsibilities of all staff involved in the recruitment process. This includes outlining who is responsible for each stage of the process.

Training and Awareness: Provide training to all involved staff on the recruitment procedures and the importance of adherence. Regularly review and reinforce procedures to ensure compliance.

Monitoring and Accountability

Process Audits: Implement regular audits and reviews of the recruitment process to ensure adherence to procedures. Address any deviations or non-compliance promptly.

Using Various Selection Methods and Assessment Tools

Diverse Methods

Selection Tools: Utilize a variety of selection methods and tools, such as structured interviews, skills assessments, psychometric tests, and work samples, to evaluate candidates comprehensively.

Assessment Criteria: Ensure that assessment tools are aligned with job requirements and organizational needs. Use these tools to objectively assess candidates' skills, qualifications, and fit for the role.

Supporting a Fair and Diverse Recruitment Process

Fair Procedures:

Equitable Practices: Implement procedures that promote fairness and prevent discrimination. This includes standardizing interview questions, using objective criteria for evaluations, and ensuring a diverse selection panel.

Diversity Initiatives: Develop and promote initiatives aimed at recruiting a diverse workforce. Ensure that job postings reach a broad audience and encourage applications from underrepresented groups.

Leveraging Staff Networks for Referrals

Referral Programs

Employee Referrals: Encourage current staff to refer candidates from their networks. This can be facilitated through an employee referral program with incentives for successful hires.

Networking Opportunities: Promote networking events and opportunities where employees can connect with potential candidates and represent the organization positively.

Considering Local/National Recruitment Platforms

Platform Utilization

Local and National Platforms: Incorporate local and national recruitment platforms such as LinkedIn, industry-specific job boards, local newspapers, and community centers into your recruitment strategy.

Targeted Outreach: Tailor job postings to specific platforms based on the role's requirements and the target candidate pool. Utilize local resources to reach candidates who may be particularly well-suited for the role.

Effective recruitment procedures are vital for ensuring that the organization attracts, selects, and hires the right talent while mitigating risks and promoting fairness. By addressing the points outlined above—such as conducting thorough checks, maintaining secure documentation, providing candidate feedback, and using diverse selection methods—organizations can enhance their recruitment practices. This comprehensive approach not only supports the hiring of qualified and diverse candidates but also contributes to a positive organizational reputation and operational success.

Job Descriptions

Job descriptions are crucial documents in any organization, as they outline the responsibilities, requirements, and expectations for each role. They serve multiple purposes, from guiding recruitment to setting performance objectives. To ensure their effectiveness and relevance, it's important to address several key aspects of job descriptions. Here's a detailed examination of these considerations:

Comprehensive Coverage

Availability of Job Descriptions

Documentation: Ensure that every role within the organization has an up-to-date job description. This includes both newly created roles and existing ones. Each job description should accurately reflect the current duties and expectations associated with the role.

Review Process: Implement a systematic process for creating and updating job descriptions. Regularly review job descriptions to ensure they align with organizational changes, role evolution, and new business needs.

Accuracy and Currency

Regular Updates

Dynamic Adjustments: Job descriptions should be regularly reviewed and updated to reflect changes in job responsibilities, organizational structure, or industry standards. This ensures that they remain relevant and accurately represent the role.

Feedback Mechanism: Establish a mechanism for employees and managers to provide feedback on job descriptions. This helps in making timely updates and maintaining accuracy.

Format and Compliance

Appropriate Format

Consistency: Use a consistent format for all job descriptions to ensure clarity and ease of use. The format should include sections such as job title, classification, salary grade, summary of responsibilities, qualifications, and competencies.

Legal Compliance: Ensure that job descriptions comply with relevant labor laws and regulations. This includes avoiding discriminatory language and ensuring that the descriptions accurately reflect the essential functions of the role.

Performance Standards and Competencies

Inclusion of Performance Standards

Clear Expectations: Job descriptions should include performance standards or key result areas (KRAs) that outline what constitutes successful performance in the role. This helps set clear expectations for employees and provides a basis for performance evaluations.

Competency Framework Linkage: Where applicable, link job descriptions to the organization's Competencies Framework. This ensures that the required competencies for each role are clearly defined and aligned with organizational goals.

Objective Setting

Performance Management: Use job descriptions to set objectives in the performance management cycle. This helps in aligning individual goals with organizational objectives and facilitates performance tracking.

Common Core Areas of Responsibility

Inclusion of Core Responsibilities

General Responsibilities: Job descriptions should include core areas of responsibility that are common across roles, such as security, safeguarding, child protection, and protection from sexual exploitation and abuse (PSEA).

Role-Specific Details: In addition to core responsibilities, job descriptions should detail specific roles and functions unique to the position. This ensures that all critical areas are covered and tailored to the role's context.

Integration with Organizational Policies

Policy Alignment: Ensure that job descriptions reflect organizational policies and standards related to core responsibilities. This includes integrating relevant safety, security, and ethical guidelines.

Best Practices for Job Descriptions

Clarity and Precision

Clear Language: Use clear, precise language to describe job responsibilities and requirements. Avoid jargon or ambiguous terms that could lead to misunderstandings.

Inclusivity

Non-Discriminatory: Ensure that job descriptions are inclusive and do not discriminate based on gender, age, ethnicity, disability, or other protected characteristics.

Engagement

Employee Involvement: Involve employees and managers in the process of creating and updating job descriptions. This helps ensure that the descriptions accurately reflect the job and meet practical needs.

Accessibility

Availability: Make job descriptions easily accessible to all employees. This can be done through an internal HR portal or shared drive.

Effective job descriptions are vital for guiding recruitment, setting performance expectations, and ensuring alignment with organizational goals. By ensuring that every role has a current, accurate, and legally compliant job description, including performance standards and core responsibilities, organizations can enhance their hiring processes, support employee development, and maintain a clear understanding of job expectations. Regular reviews and updates, along with adherence to best practices, contribute to a more effective and transparent workforce management strategy.

Onboarding

Onboarding is a critical process in integrating new employees into an organization, aiming to set them up for success and engagement from their very first day. This process goes beyond traditional HR functions, involving multiple facets of the organization to ensure a smooth transition and long-term retention. Here's an in-depth exploration of effective onboarding practices and the essential role of various stakeholders in the process:

The Importance of Effective Onboarding

First Impressions Matter

- Initial Impact: The first day and weeks of employment are crucial for forming impressions. A well-structured onboarding process demonstrates to new hires that the organization values their success and is committed to their development from the outset.
- Foundation for Success: Effective onboarding helps new employees understand their role, the organization's culture, and how they contribute to the company's goals. This foundation can significantly impact their long-term productivity and engagement.

Retention and Engagement

- Early Investment: Investing in a strong onboarding program can lead to higher employee satisfaction and retention. Employees who feel welcomed and supported are more likely to stay with the organization and be motivated in their roles.
- Reduced Turnover: A structured onboarding process can reduce turnover by addressing common issues that lead to early

resignations, such as role confusion, lack of support, and cultural misalignment.

The Role of HR in Onboarding

Consistency and Coordination

- Standardization: HR is responsible for creating a consistent onboarding framework that can be applied across the organization. This includes developing standard procedures, documentation, and training materials.
- Initial Setup: HR should coordinate the logistical aspects of onboarding, such as preparing workstations, setting up IT access, and ensuring that all necessary documentation is completed.

Orientation Programs:

- Company Overview: HR should provide new hires with a comprehensive introduction to the organization, including its mission, values, policies, and procedures.
- Compliance Training: Ensure that new employees complete mandatory training sessions, such as compliance, health and safety, and company policies.

The Critical Role of Line Managers

Direct Engagement

- First Point of Contact: Line managers are often the first direct point of contact for new employees and play a crucial role in their immediate integration into the team. Their involvement can significantly impact the new hire's experience and success.
- Role Clarification: Managers should clarify job expectations, responsibilities, and performance goals. They provide the context for how the new role fits into the team and the organization's broader objectives.

Support and Feedback

Ongoing Support: Line managers should actively support new employees by providing regular feedback, answering questions, and helping them navigate their new environment.

Performance Check-ins: Schedule regular check-ins to discuss progress, address any concerns, and provide constructive feedback. This helps new hires feel valued and supported.

Integrating Across Departments

Cross-Departmental Collaboration

- Holistic Approach: Onboarding should involve various departments beyond HR, such as IT, facilities, and the specific team where the new hire will work. Each department has a role in ensuring that new employees have everything they need to be productive.
- Departmental Introductions: Facilitate introductions to key contacts and teams across the organization. This helps new hires understand the organization's structure and build relationships.

Customized Onboarding Plans:

- Role-Specific Onboarding: Tailor onboarding programs to the specific needs of different roles and departments. This ensures that the training and integration process is relevant and effective for each position.

Continuous Improvement

Feedback and Evaluation

- Gathering Feedback: Collect feedback from new employees about their onboarding experience to identify areas for improvement. Use surveys, interviews, or focus groups to gain insights.

- Program Evaluation: Regularly review and update onboarding programs based on feedback and changing organizational needs. This helps ensure that the process remains effective and relevant.

Best Practices

- Benchmarking: Stay informed about best practices in onboarding and incorporate innovative approaches to enhance the process. This can include incorporating technology, such as onboarding platforms, and providing mentorship programs.

A successful onboarding process is essential for setting new employees up for success and enhancing long-term retention. While HR plays a critical role in designing and managing the onboarding framework, the active participation of line managers and collaboration across departments are crucial for creating a welcoming and effective onboarding experience. By engaging all relevant stakeholders, organizations can ensure that new hires are integrated smoothly, feel supported, and are aligned with the company's goals from day one. This comprehensive approach not only boosts productivity and engagement but also contributes to a positive organizational culture and improved employee retention.

Line Manager Outreach	HR should take time to sit down with the line manager of a new employee prior to their arrival to explain the importance of the onboarding process and ensure that the line manager understands that it is their responsibility to be prepared and proactive.
Pre-Arrival Preparation	When an employee arrives, they should be greeted in a way that makes them feel expected and welcome. This requires timely preparation prior to the start date.
First Day Orientation	On an employee's first day, they should meet with both HR – to review and complete essential paperwork – and their line manager to get acquainted with the job requirements, the office environment and culture, and to understand what is expected of them during their first week.

Buddy System	Setting up a 'buddy system' to pair each new employee with an existing employee (ideally someone at the similar level but from a different department) is a great way to support new hires. A buddy, or peer, can be a helpful resource to new hires for asking questions that they may not want to ask their line manager, and it is a good way for them to meet people outside their team/department.
"Day 10" Orientation	New employees often experience information overload during their first days on the job. Holding a "Day 10 Orientation" sessions can provide an opportunity for new employees to ask follow-up questions and share feedback on their experience so far. This session should be held by HR and can be about one hour depending on the number of questions employees may have.

Table 2: Onboarding

Manage

Performance Management

Implementing an effective performance management process is crucial for an organization's success, despite the challenges and time investment it requires from HR, employees, and line managers. A well-designed performance management system can significantly enhance organizational culture, boost staff morale, reduce turnover, and ensure that teams meet their objectives. Conversely, a poorly executed system can have detrimental effects, such as damaging organizational culture, lowering staff morale, increasing turnover, and impeding the achievement of goals.

The Importance of Performance Management

Performance Management Overview: Performance management is a continuous process that involves planning, monitoring, reviewing, and improving employees' work performance. A robust performance management system ensures that employees are aligned with organizational goals and are motivated to contribute their best.

Challenges and Benefits

Challenges: Implementing an effective system can be time-consuming and may require significant effort from HR, line managers, and employees. The complexity of balancing fair assessments, providing constructive feedback, and managing performance expectations can be demanding.

Benefits: When executed well, performance management can lead to increased employee engagement, better alignment with organizational goals, and improved overall performance. It helps identify high performers and areas where employees may need additional support or development.

Key Components of Performance Management

Agreement on Objectives and Plans

Objective Setting:

SMART Goals: Ensure that employees and line managers set clear, measurable, achievable, relevant, and time-bound (SMART) objectives at the beginning of the performance cycle. This helps in defining expectations and aligning individual goals with organizational objectives.

Collaborative Approach: The process should be collaborative, with employees actively participating in setting their goals. This fosters ownership and motivation.

Planning:

Action Plans: Develop detailed action plans outlining the steps needed to achieve the objectives. This includes identifying resources, timelines, and any potential obstacles.

Opportunities for Merit Increases and Promotions

Merit-Based Rewards:

Recognition and Compensation: Establish a system for merit-based increases and promotions linked to performance outcomes. This ensures that employees who meet or exceed their goals are appropriately rewarded.

Transparent Criteria: Clearly communicate the criteria for merit increases and promotions to employees. This helps them understand what is required to advance in their careers.

Regular Feedback

Continuous Feedback:

Frequent Interactions: Implement a system for providing regular feedback, rather than relying solely on annual reviews. Frequent feedback helps employees stay on track and make adjustments as needed.

Constructive Criticism: Ensure that feedback is constructive, specific, and actionable. Focus on both strengths and areas for improvement.

Performance Tracking:

Progress Monitoring: Use performance metrics and regular check-ins to track progress towards objectives. This helps in identifying any issues early and addressing them promptly.

Identifying Areas for Improvement and Development

Development Plans:

Growth Opportunities: Work with employees to identify areas where they need improvement and opportunities for growth. Develop personalized learning and development plans to address these areas.

Skill Enhancement: Offer training, workshops, or mentorship programs to help employees develop the skills needed to improve their performance and advance their careers.

Actionable Insights:

Performance Reviews: Use performance reviews to provide actionable insights into areas for improvement. Collaborate with employees to create actionable steps for development.

Career Development Planning

Career Goals:

Future Planning: Encourage employees to plan for their career development by discussing their long-term career goals and aspirations. This helps in aligning their current performance with future career opportunities.

Support Mechanisms: Provide support through career counselling, training, and job rotation opportunities to help employees achieve their career goals.

Development Pathways:

Career Pathways: Outline clear career pathways and development opportunities within the organization. This helps employees understand how they can progress and what steps they need to take.

Best Practices for Performance Management

Consistency and Fairness:

Standardized Processes: Ensure that performance management processes are consistent and fair across the organization. This includes using standardized evaluation criteria and providing equal opportunities for feedback and development.

Employee Engagement:

Active Participation: Involve employees in the performance management process. Encourage them to set their own goals, participate in feedback sessions, and take ownership of their development.

Training for Managers:

Manager Development: Train line managers in effective performance management techniques, including goal setting, providing feedback, and conducting performance reviews. Well-trained managers are better equipped to support their team members.

Technology Utilization:

Performance Management Systems: Use technology solutions, such as performance management software, to streamline the process. These tools can help with tracking goals, providing feedback, and managing performance reviews.

Continuous Improvement:

Process Review: Regularly review and refine the performance management process based on feedback from employees and managers. Continuously seek ways to improve and adapt the system to changing organizational needs.

Conclusion

Implementing a robust performance management process is essential for enhancing organizational effectiveness and employee satisfaction. By focusing on clear objective setting, providing regular feedback, offering opportunities for merit-based rewards and career development, and ensuring a collaborative approach, organizations can create a performance management system that supports both individual and organizational success. Despite the challenges, investing in a well-structured performance management system pays off by fostering a motivated, engaged, and high-performing workforce.

Compensations Management

Compensation and Benefits: The Essential Role in Total Rewards

Compensation and benefits, often collectively termed "rewards," form a fundamental component of an organization's overall HR framework. These systems and procedures not only define staff grading, salaries, and various benefits but also significantly influence an organization's ability to attract, retain, and motivate its workforce.

Understanding Compensation and Benefits

Definitions and Scope:

- Compensation: This refers to the financial remuneration employees receive for their work, including base salary, bonuses, and incentives. It is often structured based on job roles, responsibilities, and performance levels.
- Benefits: These include non-monetary rewards such as health insurance, retirement plans, paid time off, and other perks. Benefits enhance the overall employment package and contribute to employee well-being and job satisfaction.

Total Rewards Concept:

- Holistic View: Many organizations adopt a "total rewards" approach, which integrates compensation and benefits with other elements of the employment proposition. This broader perspective includes:
  - Learning and Development Opportunities: Training, professional development, and career advancement resources.

- ○ Career Development: Clear paths for growth within the organization and support for achieving long-term career goals.
- ○ Work Environment: The quality of the workplace, including safety, culture, and work-life balance.
- ○ Working Patterns: Flexible working hours, remote work options, and other arrangements that contribute to employee satisfaction.

Importance of a Well-Designed Rewards System

Attraction of Talent:

- Competitive Edge: A well-structured rewards system helps organizations attract top talent by offering competitive salaries and appealing benefits packages. This is crucial for drawing individuals who possess the passion, professionalism, and skills necessary to advance the organization's mission.
- Employer Branding: Effective rewards contribute to a strong employer brand, making the organization more attractive to prospective employees.

2. Retention and Motivation:

- Valuing Employees: An effective rewards structure motivates employees by recognizing their contributions and making them feel valued. This, in turn, enhances job satisfaction and reduces turnover rates.
- Performance Incentives: Performance-based rewards, such as bonuses and merit increases, can drive high performance by aligning employees' goals with organizational objectives.

Alignment with Organizational Goals:

- Strategic Fit: The rewards system should align with the organization's strategic goals and values. This ensures that the compensation and benefits offered support the overall mission and encourage behaviors that contribute to organizational success.

- Consistency and Fairness: Implementing a fair and consistent rewards system helps maintain equity among employees and fosters a positive organizational culture.

Key Elements of an Effective Rewards System

Competitive Compensation:

- Market Benchmarking: Regularly review and adjust salaries based on market trends and industry standards to ensure competitiveness.
- Transparent Structures: Develop clear salary bands and grading systems that are transparent and understood by all employees.

Comprehensive Benefits Package:

- Health and Wellness: Offer a robust benefits package that includes health insurance, dental and vision coverage, and wellness programs.
- Retirement Plans: Provide retirement savings plans with employer contributions or matching, ensuring financial security for employees in their later years.
- Paid Leave: Include generous paid time off policies, such as vacation days, sick leave, and parental leave, to support work-life balance.

Learning and Development:

- Training Opportunities: Invest in employees' professional growth by providing access to training, workshops, and certification programs.
- Career Pathing: Create opportunities for career advancement and skill development to help employees achieve their long-term career goals.

Work Environment and Flexibility:

- Positive Culture: Foster a positive and inclusive work environment that supports employee well-being and engagement.
- Flexible Working Arrangements: Offer options such as remote work, flexible hours, and job sharing to accommodate diverse needs and preferences.

Best Practices for Implementing a Rewards System

Regular Assessment:

- Review and Update: Continuously assess the effectiveness of the rewards system and make adjustments based on employee feedback, market changes, and organizational needs.
- Benchmarking: Compare your rewards package with industry standards to ensure it remains competitive and attractive.

Employee Communication:

- Transparency: Communicate the details of the rewards system clearly to all employees. This includes explaining how compensation is determined, the benefits available, and any performance-related incentives.
- Feedback Mechanisms: Implement channels for employees to provide feedback on the rewards system and address any concerns or suggestions.

Integration with HR Practices:

- Alignment: Ensure that the rewards system is integrated with other HR practices, such as performance management, recruitment, and employee development. This alignment helps reinforce organizational values and objectives.
- Consistency: Apply rewards practices consistently across the organization to maintain fairness and equity.

Legal and Regulatory Compliance:

- Adherence to Laws: Ensure that all aspects of the rewards system comply with local, national, and international employment laws and regulations.

A well-designed compensation and benefits system, as part of a broader "total rewards" strategy, is essential for attracting and retaining top talent, motivating employees, and aligning their efforts with organizational goals. By focusing on competitive compensation, comprehensive benefits, professional development, and a positive work environment, organizations can create a rewards system that enhances employee satisfaction, supports organizational success, and contributes to a thriving workplace culture.

Employee Relations

Employee Relations: Managing Workplace Interactions and Conflict

Employee relations encompasses the formal interactions between staff members, managers, and the organization. It is a critical area of human resources (HR) that involves supporting line managers in preventing, managing, and resolving conflicts, as well as maintaining a positive and productive work environment. Effective management of employee relations is essential for fostering a harmonious workplace, addressing issues constructively, and ensuring that performance and conduct issues are handled fairly and transparently.

Key Aspects of Employee Relations

Prevention and Management of Conflicts:

Proactive Measures:

- Training and Development: Equip line managers with training on conflict resolution, communication skills, and effective management techniques. This helps in preventing conflicts from escalating and fosters a positive work environment.

- Clear Policies: Establish and communicate clear policies regarding workplace behavior, conflict resolution, and grievance procedures. Ensuring that employees are aware of these policies can help in managing expectations and reducing conflicts.

Conflict Management:

- Mediation and Coaching: Provide support through mediation and coaching when conflicts arise. Mediation involves an impartial third party facilitating a resolution between conflicting parties, while coaching helps individuals develop skills to manage conflicts more effectively.
- Open Communication: Encourage open lines of communication between employees and managers. This helps in identifying and addressing potential issues early, before they escalate into major conflicts.

Handling Disciplinary and Grievance Procedures:

Disciplinary Actions:

- Constructive Discipline: When disciplinary actions are necessary, they should be constructive and aimed at improving performance or correcting undesirable conduct. This includes providing clear feedback, setting improvement goals, and offering support for achieving those goals.
- Fair Process: Ensure that disciplinary processes are fair, consistent, and transparent. Follow established procedures and provide employees with an opportunity to respond to allegations or performance concerns.

Grievance Management:

Grievance Policy: Implement a clear grievance policy that outlines how employees can raise concerns or complaints. Ensure that the process is accessible, confidential, and provides a fair resolution.

Resolution and Follow-Up: Address grievances promptly and thoroughly. After a resolution is reached, follow up to ensure that the issue has been resolved and that the solution is effective.

Creating a Positive Work Environment:

Transparency and Honesty:

- Clear Communication: Address performance concerns and behavioral issues in an honest and transparent manner. Clearly communicate expectations, provide constructive feedback, and involve employees in finding solutions.
- Supportive Culture: Foster a culture of support where employees feel comfortable discussing concerns and seeking help. Encourage positive interactions and collaborative problem-solving.

Performance Management:

- Regular Reviews: Conduct regular performance reviews to identify and address issues early. Use these reviews as an opportunity to provide feedback, set goals, and discuss development opportunities.
- Goal Setting: Work with employees to set clear, achievable goals and provide the necessary support and resources to help them meet these goals.

Best Practices for Effective Employee Relations:

Preventive Strategies:

- Regular Training: Offer ongoing training for managers and employees on conflict resolution, communication, and workplace behavior. Regular training helps in maintaining a positive work environment and reduces the likelihood of conflicts.
- Employee Engagement: Engage employees through surveys, feedback sessions, and team-building activities. Understanding employee concerns and fostering a sense of belonging can prevent conflicts and improve morale.

Consistent Implementation:

- Policy Adherence: Ensure that all employee relations policies and procedures are consistently applied across the organization. This includes handling conflicts, disciplinary actions, and grievances in a fair and uniform manner.
- Documentation: Keep detailed records of all employee relations activities, including conflicts, disciplinary actions, and grievances. Proper documentation helps in tracking issues, ensuring compliance, and supporting decisions.

Support Systems:

- HR Support: Provide HR support to line managers in managing complex or sensitive issues. HR can offer guidance, mediation, and resources to help resolve conflicts effectively.
- Employee Assistance Programs (EAPs): Implement EAPs to provide employees with access to counselling and support services for personal and professional issues. EAPs can help employees manage stress, resolve conflicts, and improve overall well-being.

Effective employee relations are essential for maintaining a positive and productive work environment. By proactively managing conflicts, implementing fair disciplinary and grievance procedures, and fostering open communication, organizations can address performance concerns and behavioral issues constructively. HR plays a crucial role in supporting line managers, ensuring consistency in handling employee relations matters, and creating an environment where employees feel valued and supported. Adopting best practices and focusing on transparency, fairness, and support can lead to a more harmonious workplace and contribute to overall organizational success.

Inspire

Learning & Development

Learning and Development: Enhancing Employee Growth and Organizational Success

Learning and development (L&D) is a strategic process that focuses on equipping staff with the skills, knowledge, and capabilities needed to contribute effectively to organizational goals. It involves creating opportunities for employees to engage in continuous learning, develop professionally, and enhance their performance. This commitment to L&D not only supports individual growth but also drives overall organizational success and fosters a culture of continuous improvement.

Key Aspects of Learning and Development

Aligning with Organizational Goals:

Understanding Objectives:

- Organizational Alignment: Ensure that employees understand and are committed to the organization's mission, values, and strategic objectives. L&D programs should be designed to align with these goals, helping employees see how their roles contribute to the broader organizational purpose.

- Clear Communication: Regularly communicate the organization's goals and how individual learning and development efforts support these objectives. This helps employees connect their personal growth with the organization's success.

Commitment to Learning:

- Ownership of Learning: Encourage employees to take ownership of their learning journey. Provide them with resources and support to pursue continuous development, including reskilling and upskilling opportunities throughout their tenure.

  - Personal Development Plans: Work with employees to create personalized development plans that align with their career goals and the organization's needs.

Promoting Engagement and Participation:

Collaborative Learning:

- Team and Partner Collaboration: Facilitate opportunities for employees to work with colleagues, partners, and beneficiaries in ways that promote learning and active participation. Collaborative projects and cross-functional teams can enhance knowledge sharing and skill development.
- Interactive Learning: Implement interactive and participatory learning methods, such as workshops, seminars, and group discussions, to engage employees and encourage active involvement.

Encouraging Knowledge Sharing:

- Sharing Lessons: Foster a culture where employees are encouraged to share their experiences and lessons learned both within and outside the organization. This contributes to a learning organization where knowledge is continuously shared and applied.

Enhancing Work Effectiveness:

Assessment and Planning:

- Performance Reviews: Regularly assess and review employees' work to identify areas for improvement and development. Use this feedback to plan targeted training and development initiatives.
- Setting Standards: Establish high standards for work performance and ensure that training programs are designed to help employees meet and exceed these standards.

Continuous Improvement:

- Feedback Mechanisms: Implement mechanisms for ongoing feedback and evaluation of L&D programs. Use this feedback to refine training initiatives and ensure they effectively address employees' needs.

Professional Development and Organizational Impact:

Influence on Attraction and Retention:

- Employee Attraction: A strong commitment to professional development enhances the organization's ability to attract top talent. Prospective employees are often drawn to organizations that offer opportunities for growth and career advancement.
- Retention: Investing in employees' professional development contributes to higher job satisfaction and retention. Employees are more likely to stay with an organization that supports their career growth and development.

Building Capabilities:

- Skill Development: Well-designed training sessions contribute to organizational learning by developing employees' skills and capabilities. This, in turn, strengthens the organization's overall performance and ability to achieve its mission.

Creating a Learning Organization:

Culture of Learning:

- Learning Environment: Create an environment that supports and encourages continuous learning. This includes providing access to resources, training programs, and opportunities for employees to develop their skills.
- Recognition and Reward: Recognize and reward employees who actively engage in learning and development. This reinforces the importance of professional growth and motivates others to participate.

Adapting to Change:

- Continuous Adaptation: In today's fast-paced and evolving work environment, organizations must be agile and adaptive. A commitment to learning and development ensures that employees can adapt to changes and challenges, keeping the organization competitive and resilient.

Best Practices for Implementing Learning and Development Programs

Align Training with Business Needs:

- Needs Assessment: Conduct regular assessments to identify skills gaps and training needs that align with the organization's strategic goals.
- Targeted Programs: Develop training programs that address specific needs and priorities, ensuring they are relevant and impactful.

Utilize Diverse Learning Methods:

- Blended Learning: Incorporate a mix of learning methods, including online courses, in-person workshops, coaching, and mentoring, to accommodate different learning styles and preferences.
- On-the-Job Learning: Encourage experiential learning through on-the-job training, job rotations, and project-based assignments.

Foster a Supportive Learning Culture:

- Management Support: Ensure that leaders and managers actively support and participate in L&D initiatives. Their involvement is crucial for creating a culture that values learning and development.
- Encouragement and Support: Provide employees with the necessary support and encouragement to pursue their learning goals, including time and resources for training.

Measure and Evaluate Effectiveness:

- Tracking Progress: Use metrics and evaluation tools to track the effectiveness of L&D programs. Assess employee progress, learning outcomes, and the impact on organizational performance.
- Continuous Improvement: Use evaluation results to continuously improve and refine L&D initiatives. Adapt programs based on feedback and changing organizational needs.

Promote Career Development:

- Career Pathways: Develop clear career pathways and growth opportunities within the organization. Support employees in planning and achieving their career goals.
- Mentorship and Coaching: Offer mentorship and coaching programs to provide guidance and support for employees' professional development.

Learning and development are vital for enhancing employee performance, fostering a culture of continuous improvement, and achieving organizational success. By aligning L&D programs with organizational goals, promoting engagement and participation, and creating a supportive learning environment, organizations can ensure that their staff is equipped with the skills and knowledge needed to excel. Investing in professional development not only enhances individual capabilities but also strengthens the organization's ability to achieve its mission and maintain a competitive edge.

Engagement

Employee Engagement: The Key to Organizational Success and Job Satisfaction

Employee engagement is a critical driver of organizational success and job satisfaction. It encompasses the conditions and practices that enable employees to give their best every day, align with the organization's goals and values, and feel motivated and committed to contributing to overall success. High levels of employee engagement result in a more productive, creative, and loyal workforce, which is essential for achieving organizational objectives and fostering a positive work environment.

Understanding Employee Engagement

Definition and Importance:

- Definition: Employee engagement refers to the level of enthusiasm, commitment, and involvement an employee has towards their role and the organization. Engaged employees are deeply connected to their work and the organization's mission, and they consistently put forth discretionary effort to achieve organizational goals.
- Importance: Engagement is directly linked to job satisfaction and organizational performance. When employees are engaged, they

are more likely to perform at their best, contribute innovative ideas, and remain committed to the organization. Conversely, disengaged employees may exhibit lower productivity, reduced creativity, and a higher likelihood of turnover.

Components of Employee Engagement:

Commitment to Organizational Goals:

- Alignment: Engaged employees understand and align with the organization's goals and values. They see how their individual roles contribute to the larger mission and purpose of the organization.
- Motivation: Employees are motivated by a sense of purpose and are eager to contribute to the success of the organization.

Wellbeing and Satisfaction:

- Job Satisfaction: High engagement levels are closely tied to job satisfaction. Employees who are engaged feel fulfilled and satisfied with their roles, which positively impacts their overall wellbeing.
- Work-Life Balance: Ensuring a healthy work-life balance is crucial for maintaining employee engagement and preventing burnout.

The Impact of Employee Engagement

Productivity and Performance:

- Enhanced Productivity: Engaged employees are more productive because they are committed to achieving high performance and are motivated to exceed expectations. They are also more likely to go the extra mile in their work.
- Improved Quality: Higher engagement levels lead to better quality work, as engaged employees take pride in their contributions and strive for excellence.

Creativity and Innovation:

- Innovation: Engaged employees are more likely to contribute innovative ideas and solutions. Their enthusiasm for their work often translates into creative thinking and problem-solving.
- Continuous Improvement: Engaged employees actively seek ways to improve processes and contribute to the organization's success through continuous learning and development.

Loyalty and Retention:

- Employee Retention: High engagement levels are associated with increased employee loyalty and reduced turnover. Engaged employees are more likely to stay with the organization and invest in their long-term success.
- Reduced Absenteeism: Engaged employees are less likely to miss work or exhibit disengaged behavior, which helps maintain consistent productivity levels.

Strategies for Enhancing Employee Engagement

Create a Positive Work Environment:

- Supportive Culture: Foster a work culture that values employee contributions, promotes mutual respect, and encourages collaboration. A positive work environment enhances employee morale and engagement.
- Recognition and Rewards: Regularly recognize and reward employees for their hard work and achievements. Acknowledgment of their efforts reinforces their commitment and motivation.

Provide Opportunities for Growth:

- Career Development: Offer opportunities for professional growth and career advancement. Employees are more engaged when they see a clear path for their development within the organization.

- Training and Development: Invest in training and development programs that enhance employees' skills and knowledge. This investment demonstrates a commitment to their growth and fosters engagement.

Encourage Open Communication:

- Feedback Mechanisms: Implement regular feedback mechanisms to understand employees' perspectives and address their concerns. Open communication helps build trust and ensures that employees feel heard and valued.
- Transparent Leadership: Maintain transparency in organizational decisions and changes. When employees are informed and involved in decision-making, they are more likely to feel engaged and invested.

Support Work-Life Balance:

- Flexible Work Arrangements: Provide flexible working options, such as remote work or flexible hours, to help employees balance their work and personal lives. This flexibility contributes to their overall well-being and engagement.
- Wellbeing Programs: Offer programs and resources that support employees' physical and mental health. Initiatives such as wellness programs, mental health support, and work-life balance initiatives enhance employee satisfaction and engagement.

Align Roles with Strengths:

- Role Fit: Ensure that employees are in roles that align with their skills and strengths. When employees are well-matched to their roles, they are more likely to feel engaged and perform at their best.
- Personal Development: Support employees in identifying their strengths and interests and align their roles and responsibilities accordingly.

Measuring and Evaluating Engagement

Engagement Surveys:

- Regular Assessment: Conduct regular employee engagement surveys to assess engagement levels, identify areas for improvement, and gather feedback on employees' experiences.
- Actionable Insights: Use survey results to make informed decisions and implement changes that address employee concerns and enhance engagement.

Performance Metrics:

- Monitor Key Metrics: Track key performance metrics such as productivity, turnover rates, and absenteeism to evaluate the impact of engagement initiatives and identify trends.
- Continuous Improvement: Use performance data to continuously improve engagement strategies and ensure they are effectively meeting employee needs.

Employee engagement is essential for organizational success and job satisfaction. By creating a supportive work environment, providing opportunities for growth, encouraging open communication, supporting work-life balance, and aligning roles with employees' strengths, organizations can foster high levels of engagement. Engaged employees are more productive, innovative, and loyal, contributing significantly to the overall success of the organization. Measuring and evaluating engagement levels helps ensure that strategies are effective and allows for continuous improvement in fostering a motivated and committed workforce.

Recognition

The Importance of Effective Employee Recognition: Best Practices and Guidelines

Employee recognition is the practice of acknowledging and appreciating employees for their contributions and achievements.

Effective recognition not only boosts employee morale but also enhances productivity, loyalty, and overall well-being. Research consistently shows that when employees feel valued and recognized for their efforts, they are more engaged, motivated, and committed to their roles. To implement a successful recognition program, it's essential to follow key best practices that ensure fairness, relevance, and meaningful impact.

Best Practices for Employee Recognition

Ensure Fairness in Recognition:

Genuine Effort and Achievement:

- Merit-Based Recognition: Awards and recognition should be based on genuine accomplishments and efforts. It's crucial to acknowledge the specific contributions that have made a significant impact, rather than recognizing employees for reasons unrelated to their performance.
- Avoid Favoritism: Recognition should not be influenced by favoritism or internal politics. Implement objective criteria for evaluating achievements to ensure that all employees have an equal opportunity to be recognized based on their performance and contributions.

Cultural Sensitivity:

- Local Customs and Culture: Design recognition programs that are sensitive to local customs and cultural norms. What is considered appropriate and meaningful can vary greatly across different regions and cultures, so tailor recognition practices to fit the diverse backgrounds of your employees.

Avoid Fixed Schedules for Awards:

Avoid Predictability:

- Timing and Authenticity: Recognitions should not be tied to a fixed schedule, such as monthly awards, as this can lead to perceptions of insincerity. When awards are distributed according to a set timetable, they may appear forced or routine rather than a genuine acknowledgment of exceptional performance.
- Timely Recognition: Instead, provide recognition in a timely manner, closely following the achievement or contribution. Immediate acknowledgment reinforces the connection between the effort and the recognition, making it more meaningful and impactful.

Design Equitable Recognition Programs:

Merit-Based Distribution:

- Recognize Based on Merit: Ensure that recognition is distributed based on merit and achievement. It's natural for some employees to be recognized more frequently than others, and this disparity reflects their varying levels of contributions and performance.
- Meaningful Recognition: If everyone receives equal recognition, the value of the acknowledgment diminishes. Tailoring recognition to those who have made notable contributions ensures that it retains its significance and continues to drive engagement.

Program Design:

- Clear Criteria: Develop clear and transparent criteria for recognition to ensure that employees understand what behaviors and achievements are being rewarded. This clarity helps align employee efforts with organizational goals and standards.

- Variety of Recognition Forms: Offer a variety of recognition forms, such as verbal praise, written commendations, monetary rewards, or additional time off, to cater to different preferences and ensure that recognition feels personal and meaningful.

Impact of Effective Employee Recognition

Enhanced Productivity and Motivation:

- Increased Motivation: Employees who feel recognized are more motivated to maintain high performance and contribute to organizational goals. Recognized employees often exhibit greater enthusiasm and commitment to their work.
- Boosted Productivity: Effective recognition can lead to increased productivity as employees strive to meet and exceed the standards set by their recognition programs.

Improved Employee Loyalty and Retention:

- Increased Loyalty: When employees feel appreciated, they are more likely to develop a sense of loyalty to the organization. This loyalty can translate into longer tenure and reduced turnover rates.
- Retention Benefits: Recognition programs can be a powerful tool for retaining top talent, as employees who feel valued are less likely to seek opportunities elsewhere.

3. Reduced Stress and Increased Job Satisfaction:

- Lower Stress Levels: Recognition contributes to a positive work environment, which can help reduce stress and improve overall job satisfaction. Employees who feel acknowledged for their efforts are less likely to experience burnout.
- Enhanced Well-being: Acknowledgment and appreciation contribute to an employee's sense of well-being, making them more engaged and satisfied with their job.

Implementing an Effective Recognition Program

Define Objectives and Criteria:

- Program Objectives: Clearly define the objectives of your recognition program, including what behaviors and achievements you want to encourage and how you will measure success.
- Recognition Criteria: Establish criteria for recognition that are aligned with organizational goals and values. Ensure that these criteria are communicated clearly to all employees.

Communicate and Train:

- Program Communication: Clearly communicate the details of the recognition program to all employees. Make sure they understand how the program works and how they can earn recognition.
- Training for Managers: Provide training for managers on how to effectively recognize and reward employees. Managers should be equipped to offer meaningful and timely recognition.

Monitor and Evaluate:

- Regular Monitoring: Regularly monitor the effectiveness of the recognition program. Collect feedback from employees and assess the impact on engagement, performance, and satisfaction.
- Continuous Improvement: Use feedback and performance data to make necessary adjustments to the program. Continuously improve the recognition practices to ensure they remain relevant and impactful.

Effective employee recognition is a powerful tool for enhancing productivity, motivation, and job satisfaction. By ensuring fairness, avoiding fixed schedules, and designing equitable programs, organizations can create meaningful recognition practices that drive employee engagement and contribute to overall success. Recognizing and valuing employee contributions not only fosters a positive work environment but also strengthens loyalty, reduces stress, and improves organizational performance. Implementing and continuously refining a robust recognition program can significantly enhance the overall effectiveness of your workforce and support your organization's long-term goals.

Care

Health, Safety, and Security

Establishing a Robust Health and Safety Policy: Key Components and Responsibilities

In any organization, the establishment of a comprehensive health and safety policy is crucial for safeguarding employees and ensuring their well-being while they perform their duties. This policy should include accident reporting procedures and risk management practices to address potential hazards and minimize risks. Employers have both legal obligations and a moral duty of care to create and maintain a safe and healthy work environment. An effective approach to fulfilling these responsibilities includes integrating a staff health program into the organization's reward and benefit package.

Key Components of a Health and Safety Policy

Comprehensive Policy Development:

- Policy Creation: Develop a detailed health and safety policy that outlines the organization's commitment to maintaining a safe work environment. This policy should clearly define the roles and responsibilities of both employers and employees in ensuring health and safety.
- Legal Compliance: Ensure the policy complies with relevant local, national, and international regulations and standards. Regularly review and update the policy to reflect changes in laws or industry best practices.

Accident Reporting Procedures:

- Clear Reporting Process: Establish a clear and straightforward procedure for reporting accidents and incidents. Employees should know how to report an accident, whom to contact, and what information is required.
- Documentation and Investigation: Implement a system for documenting accidents and incidents, including details of the event, the individuals involved, and any immediate actions taken. Conduct thorough investigations to identify causes and prevent recurrence.

Risk Management Practices:

- Risk Assessment: Regularly conduct risk assessments to identify potential hazards in the workplace. This involves evaluating the likelihood and severity of risks and implementing appropriate controls to mitigate them.
- Preventive Measures: Develop and implement preventive measures and safety protocols based on the findings of risk assessments. These measures should address identified risks and aim to minimize their impact.

Training and Awareness:

- Employee Training: Provide training to employees on health and safety procedures, including how to report accidents, use safety equipment, and follow emergency protocols. Regular refresher courses should be conducted to keep employees informed of any updates or changes.
- Management Training: Train managers and supervisors on their responsibilities regarding health and safety, including how to enforce policies and handle incidents effectively.

Legal and Ethical Responsibilities

Legal Liability:

- Compliance with Laws: Employers are legally obligated to comply with occupational health and safety laws. Failure to adhere to these regulations can result in legal consequences, including fines, sanctions, and potential lawsuits.
- Duty of Care: Beyond legal requirements, employers have a duty of care to protect their employees' health and safety. This involves proactively addressing potential hazards and ensuring that the workplace is free from unreasonable risks.

Ethical Duty:

- Employee Well-being: Ensuring employee safety is not just a legal obligation but also an ethical responsibility. A safe working environment demonstrates respect for employees and contributes to their overall job satisfaction and morale.

Incorporating Health Programs into Reward and Benefit Packages

Health Programs as Benefits:

- Staff Health Programs: Integrate health and wellness programs into the organization's reward and benefit package. This can include offering health insurance, wellness initiatives, mental health support, and fitness programs.
- Preventive Health Measures: Encourage preventive health measures, such as regular health screenings, vaccinations, and health education, to promote overall well-being and reduce the incidence of work-related illnesses.

Enhancing Employee Engagement:

- Wellness Incentives: Provide incentives for employees who actively participate in health and wellness programs. This can include discounts on health-related services, rewards for achieving wellness goals, or recognition for participation in health initiatives.

- Creating a Healthy Culture: Foster a culture that values and supports employee health. Promote wellness as a key aspect of the organizational culture and encourage employees to prioritize their well-being.

Monitoring and Evaluating Health and Safety Measures

Continuous Monitoring:

- Regular Inspections: Conduct regular workplace inspections to ensure compliance with health and safety policies. Address any identified issues promptly to maintain a safe work environment.
- Employee Feedback: Gather feedback from employees regarding health and safety practices and make improvements based on their input. Encourage open communication about safety concerns and suggestions.

Evaluation and Improvement:

- Assess Effectiveness: Regularly evaluate the effectiveness of health and safety policies and programs. Use data from accident reports, risk assessments, and employee feedback to identify areas for improvement.
- Continuous Improvement: Implement changes and improvements to enhance health and safety measures. Stay informed about new safety technologies, practices, and regulations to keep the organization's policies up-to-date.

Establishing and maintaining a robust health and safety policy is essential for protecting employees and ensuring a productive and secure work environment. Employers must develop comprehensive policies, implement effective accident reporting and risk management procedures, and integrate health programs into their reward and benefit packages. By fulfilling legal and ethical responsibilities and continuously monitoring and improving health and safety practices, organizations can create a safe and supportive workplace that contributes to overall employee well-being and organizational success.

Stress at work and staff wellbeing

Enhancing Staff Wellbeing in Nonprofit, Humanitarian, and Development Organizations

In nonprofit, humanitarian, and development organizations, staff often work in challenging environments that include multicultural teams, high-stress situations, and insecure settings. These conditions can lead to heightened stress levels, particularly when combined with limited access to private spaces and recreational activities. Such stress can adversely affect both individual performance and team effectiveness, potentially undermining the organization's overall mission and security. It is essential for HR managers to prioritize staff care and wellbeing to maintain a productive and healthy workforce.

Understanding the Impact of Stress

Stress in High-Stress Environments:

- Multicultural and High-Stress Settings: Working in multicultural teams and high-stress environments requires staff to navigate diverse cultural norms while handling intense workloads and challenging situations. These factors can exacerbate stress, leading to burnout and decreased job satisfaction.
- Limited Resources and Facilities: The lack of private spaces and leisure activities compounds stress. Employees who are already under significant pressure may find it difficult to unwind or find respite from their demanding roles.

2. Consequences of Ignoring Staff Wellbeing:

- Impact on Performance: Prolonged stress can impair cognitive functions, decision-making abilities, and overall performance. Employees may struggle to meet their responsibilities effectively, leading to decreased productivity.

- Team Dynamics: High stress can strain team dynamics, leading to conflicts, reduced collaboration, and a weakened sense of camaraderie. This can further disrupt organizational effectiveness and morale.

- Organizational Security: Stress-related issues can also impact the security and safety of operations, particularly in high-risk environments where attention to detail and well-being are crucial.

HR's Role in Supporting Staff Wellbeing

Coordinating Staff Care Initiatives:

- Collaboration with Leadership: HR managers should work closely with the leadership team and relevant departments to design and implement staff care initiatives. This collaboration ensures that wellbeing programs are aligned with the organization's needs and resources.

- Support Programs: Develop and promote support programs that address both physical and psychological health. This can include counseling services, stress management workshops, and wellness programs.

Encouraging Adequate Rest and Recreation:

- Promoting Breaks: HR managers should remind line managers to encourage their team members to take regular breaks for rest and recreation. Adequate downtime is essential for maintaining mental health and sustaining high levels of productivity.

- Work-Life Balance: Advocate for policies that support work-life balance, such as flexible working hours and the option to work remotely where possible. Ensuring staff have time to recharge is vital for long-term effectiveness.

Implementing Stress Management Strategies:

- Training and Resources: Provide training on stress management techniques and resources for employees. This can include workshops on mindfulness, resilience building, and time management.
- Access to Support Services: Ensure that staff have access to mental health support services and create an environment where seeking help is encouraged and normalized.

Creating a Supportive Work Environment:

- Fostering Open Communication: Promote a culture of openness where employees feel comfortable discussing their stress and wellbeing concerns. Open communication can help identify issues early and address them proactively.
- Recognition and Rewards: Regularly recognize and reward staff contributions. Acknowledgement and appreciation can help mitigate feelings of stress and improve overall job satisfaction.

Best Practices for HR Managers

Regular Check-Ins:

- Monitoring Wellbeing: Conduct regular check-ins with staff to assess their wellbeing and address any concerns they may have. This proactive approach can help identify stressors and provide timely support.

Providing Adequate Resources:

- Resource Allocation: Ensure that staff have access to necessary resources and facilities that can alleviate stress, such as relaxation areas, wellness programs, and recreational activities.

- Resourceful Environments: Create environments that promote physical and mental health, including ergonomic workspaces and opportunities for physical activity.

Developing Comprehensive Policies:

- Wellbeing Policies: Develop and implement comprehensive wellbeing policies that address both mental and physical health. Ensure that these policies are communicated effectively and are accessible to all employees.
- Crisis Management: Have crisis management procedures in place to support staff during particularly stressful periods or emergencies. This includes providing immediate support and addressing any emerging issues.

Addressing staff wellbeing in nonprofit, humanitarian, and development organizations is crucial for maintaining a healthy and effective workforce. HR managers play a key role in supporting staff through coordinated care initiatives, promoting adequate rest and recreation, and implementing stress management strategies. By prioritizing staff care and creating a supportive work environment, organizations can enhance productivity, improve team dynamics, and ensure the overall success and security of their missions. The wellbeing of staff should never be underestimated, as it directly impacts their performance, engagement, and the organization's ability to achieve its goals.

Exit

Managing Employee Exit: A Comprehensive Guide to the Final Stage of the Employee Lifecycle

The exit stage marks the conclusion of an employee's tenure with an organization, whether it is due to retirement, resignation, termination, or other reasons such as layoffs or the end of a contract. This stage, while often seen as a natural conclusion, is critical for both the departing employee and the organization. Properly managing the exit process ensures that all necessary formalities are completed, and it provides an opportunity to acknowledge and appreciate the contributions of the departing staff member.

Key Aspects of the Employee Exit Process

Understanding the Reasons for Exit:

- Voluntary Exits: These include resignations, retirements, and end-of-contract scenarios where the employee chooses to leave the organization.
- Involuntary Exits: These involve layoffs, terminations, or reductions in staffing due to organizational changes or performance issues.

The Importance of a Structured Exit Process:

An organized exit process helps ensure that all formalities are handled efficiently and consistently. This minimizes disruptions to the organization and helps maintain a positive relationship with the departing employee. Properly managing this stage also provides valuable insights for improving organizational practices and employee satisfaction.

Core HR Processes for Employee Exit

Exit Checklist:

- An Exit Checklist is a crucial tool for managing the departure of employees. It serves to ensure that all required steps are followed and that both the employee and the organization complete necessary tasks. The checklist should include:
- Finance: Final paycheck, outstanding reimbursements, and any other financial settlements.

- IT: Return of company equipment, deactivation of access to systems and networks, and retrieval of personal data from company devices.
- Administration: Termination of benefits, updating records, and processing any remaining administrative paperwork.
- HR: Conducting exit interviews, collecting feedback, and ensuring that all legal and compliance requirements are met.

Exit Interviews:

Conducting an exit interview provides an opportunity for the departing employee to share their experiences and feedback. This can offer valuable insights into the organization's strengths and areas for improvement. Key areas to address include:

- Employee Experience: Understanding the reasons for their departure, their views on the work environment, and any challenges they faced.
- Suggestions for Improvement: Gathering feedback on organizational practices, management, and work culture.
- Final Thoughts: Allowing the employee to express their thoughts and receive any final acknowledgments or goodbyes.

Administrative Formalities:

Ensure that all administrative tasks are completed:

- Document Collection: Gather all company property, such as ID badges, keys, and equipment.
- Benefits Termination: Address the termination or transfer of benefits, such as health insurance, retirement plans, and any other employee perks.
- Record Updates: Update employee records to reflect the departure and file the completed exit checklist in the employee's personnel file.

Legal and Compliance Considerations:

Ensure that the exit process complies with legal requirements and organizational policies:

- Employment Laws: Adhere to labor laws regarding final pay, termination procedures, and any applicable severance packages.
- Confidentiality Agreements: Remind the departing employee of any confidentiality agreements or non-compete clauses they are bound by.

Best Practices for Managing Employee Exit

Clear Communication:

- Notification: Clearly communicate the exit process to the departing employee, outlining what they need to do and what the organization will handle.
- Transition Planning: Develop a transition plan to manage the transfer of duties and responsibilities to other team members.

Positive Closure:

- Acknowledgment: Recognize and thank the departing employee for their contributions to the organization.
- Farewell: Organize a farewell event or gesture to provide a positive closure to their tenure, reinforcing a sense of appreciation and goodwill.

Record Keeping:

File Maintenance: Ensure that all exit documentation, including the completed checklist and exit interview notes, are filed accurately in the employee's personnel file.

Data Retention: Maintain records in accordance with legal requirements and organizational policies for future reference and compliance.

Effectively managing the exit stage of the employee lifecycle is essential for both the departing staff member and the organization. By implementing a structured exit process, including an exit checklist, conducting exit interviews, and addressing all administrative and legal formalities, HR can ensure a smooth transition and maintain positive relationships. Recognizing the contributions of departing employees and handling their exit with care reflects the organization's commitment to respect and professionalism, while also providing valuable feedback for continuous improvement.

How to monitor the HRBP team's Performance

Monitoring the performance of the HR Business Partner (HRBP) team is crucial for assessing the effectiveness of human capital management (HCM) practices within an organization. A robust evaluation framework enables organizations to identify strengths and weaknesses in their HCM strategies, making it possible to align these practices with overall organizational goals. This comprehensive approach involves evaluating various HCM practices across five broad driver categories. One key category to focus on is leadership practices, as effective leadership is critical for successful HRBP performance.

Leadership Practices and Their Impact on HRBP Performance

- Effective leadership is integral to optimizing HRBP performance. Here's how to monitor and assess leadership practices that influence HRBPs:

Open and Effective Communication

Assessment Criteria:

- Clarity and Transparency: Evaluate how well management communicates organizational goals, changes, and expectations to HRBPs. Effective communication should be clear, transparent, and timely.

- Feedback Mechanisms: Assess whether HRBPs receive regular, constructive feedback from management regarding their performance and areas for improvement.

Monitoring Methods:

- Surveys and Feedback: Conduct surveys to gather feedback from HRBPs about the effectiveness of communication from management. Analyze responses to identify areas for improvement.
- Meeting Observations: Observe regular meetings and communications between management and HRBPs to evaluate the openness and effectiveness of the dialogue.

Collaboration and Input Invitation

Assessment Criteria:

- Involvement in Decision-Making: Determine the extent to which management involves HRBPs in decision-making processes and seeks their input on HR-related matters.
- Collaborative Projects: Evaluate the frequency and quality of collaborative projects between HRBPs and other departments.

Monitoring Methods:

- Feedback Collection: Solicit feedback from HRBPs on how collaborative the management team is and how their input is valued and incorporated.
- Project Reviews: Review collaborative projects to assess the level of HRBP involvement and the outcomes of their contributions.

Elimination of Barriers and Provision of Feedback

Assessment Criteria:

- Barrier Removal: Assess how effectively management identifies and removes obstacles that hinder HRBPs' ability to perform their roles efficiently.

- Feedback Quality: Evaluate the quality and timeliness of feedback provided by managers to HRBPs. Feedback should be constructive and aimed at improving performance.

Monitoring Methods:

- Barrier Identification: Track and document instances where barriers have been identified and removed. Measure the impact of these actions on HRBP performance.
- Feedback Assessment: Use feedback tools or interviews to gauge the effectiveness and constructiveness of feedback provided to HRBPs.

Inspiration and Confidence Building

Assessment Criteria:

- Inspiration Levels: Evaluate how well managers inspire confidence and motivate HRBPs. This includes assessing motivational techniques and the ability to build trust.
- Confidence in Leadership: Measure HRBPs' confidence in their leadership and their perception of the support they receive from senior executives.

Monitoring Methods:

- Surveys and Interviews: Conduct surveys or interviews with HRBPs to assess their level of confidence in their leaders and the impact of leadership on their motivation.
- Leadership Assessments: Use leadership assessment tools to evaluate the effectiveness of senior executives in inspiring and motivating HRBPs.

Effectiveness of Leadership Development and Transition Systems

Assessment Criteria:

- Development Programs: Assess the effectiveness of leadership development programs in preparing HRBPs for future roles and responsibilities.
- Transition Management: Evaluate how well the organization manages leadership transitions and prepares HRBPs for new roles.

Monitoring Methods:

- Program Evaluation: Review the content, delivery, and outcomes of leadership development programs. Measure the impact of these programs on HRBP performance.
- Transition Reviews: Analyze the effectiveness of leadership transition processes and their impact on HRBPs' readiness for new roles.

Additional HCM Practices to Monitor

- While leadership practices are crucial, it is also important to monitor other HCM practices across different categories:

Talent Management and Development:

- Recruitment and Selection: Evaluate the effectiveness of recruitment processes in hiring suitable candidates for HRBP roles.
- Training and Development: Assess the quality and impact of training programs designed for HRBPs.

Performance Management:

- Goal Setting: Monitor how effectively goals are set for HRBPs and whether they are aligned with organizational objectives.

- Performance Reviews: Evaluate the fairness and comprehensiveness of performance reviews for HRBPs.

Employee Engagement:

- Engagement Surveys: Conduct surveys to measure HRBPs' engagement levels and their alignment with organizational goals.
- Retention Rates: Track retention rates of HRBPs and analyze factors contributing to employee turnover.

Compensation and Benefits:

- Compensation Analysis: Assess the competitiveness and fairness of compensation packages for HRBPs.
- Benefits Utilization: Monitor the utilization of benefits and their impact on HRBPs' job satisfaction.

Monitoring the performance of the HRBP team involves evaluating various leadership and HCM practices that impact their effectiveness. By focusing on open communication, collaboration, barrier removal, inspiration, and leadership development, organizations can ensure that HRBPs are well-supported and motivated. Additionally, assessing other HCM practices such as talent management, performance management, employee engagement, and compensation helps in creating a comprehensive view of HRBP performance. Regular evaluations and feedback mechanisms are essential for continuous improvement and aligning HRBP practices with organizational goals.

Employee engagement

Employee engagement is a crucial factor in organizational success, reflecting the level of commitment, enthusiasm, and involvement employees have towards their work and the organization. High levels of engagement lead to improved productivity, job satisfaction, and retention rates. Monitoring and enhancing employee engagement involves evaluating several key factors that contribute to a positive and motivating work environment. Below, we explore these factors and provide strategies for assessment and improvement.

Key Factors Influencing Employee Engagement

Effective Work Organization and Skill Utilization

Assessment Criteria:

- Skill Alignment: Evaluate whether employees' roles are designed to make full use of their skills and expertise. Jobs should be structured in a way that leverages the strengths of each employee.
- Work Organization: Assess how well the work is organized to ensure efficiency and effectiveness. This includes clear role definitions, manageable workloads, and proper resource allocation.

Monitoring Methods:

- Employee Feedback: Use surveys or interviews to gather employees' perspectives on how well their skills are utilized and how the organization supports effective work organization.
- Performance Metrics: Analyze performance data to see if there are correlations between skill utilization and productivity levels. Review if employees' skills are aligned with their job responsibilities.

Job Security, Recognition, and Career Advancement

Assessment Criteria:

- Job Security: Assess employees' perceptions of job stability and whether they feel secure in their positions. Job security is fundamental to reducing anxiety and fostering a positive work environment.

- Recognition: Evaluate the effectiveness of recognition programs in acknowledging employee contributions. Recognition should be timely, specific, and meaningful.
- Career Advancement: Review opportunities for career progression and development within the organization. Employees should have clear pathways for advancement and growth.

Monitoring Methods:

- Engagement Surveys: Conduct surveys to measure employees' feelings about job security, recognition, and advancement opportunities.
- Recognition Programs: Review the frequency and quality of recognition and reward programs. Collect feedback on their impact on employee motivation and engagement.

Workload Management and Work/Life Balance

Assessment Criteria:

- Workload Balance: Assess whether employees' workloads are manageable and conducive to producing high-quality work. Overburdened employees may struggle with performance and engagement.
- Work/Life Balance: Evaluate the extent to which employees can balance their work responsibilities with personal life. A healthy work/life balance is crucial for long-term engagement and job satisfaction.

Monitoring Methods:

- Workload Surveys: Use surveys to gauge employees' perceptions of their workload and whether it allows them to perform their jobs effectively.
- Work/Life Balance Assessments: Measure employees' satisfaction with their work/life balance through regular surveys

or interviews. Review the effectiveness of policies and programs designed to support work/life balance.

Ongoing Evaluation of Employee Engagement

Assessment Criteria:

- Continuous Monitoring: Ensure that employee engagement is not evaluated only at specific intervals but is continuously assessed to address issues proactively.
- Feedback Mechanisms: Implement mechanisms for regular feedback from employees about their engagement levels and any concerns they may have.

Monitoring Methods:

- Regular Surveys: Conduct regular engagement surveys to track changes in employee attitudes and identify emerging issues.
- Focus Groups: Use focus groups to gain deeper insights into employee engagement and to discuss specific areas of concern or improvement.

Strategies for Enhancing Employee Engagement

1. Foster Open Communication:

   o Encourage open and honest communication between employees and management. Regularly update employees on organizational changes and seek their input on various matters.

2. Recognize and Reward Contributions:

   o Develop a recognition program that celebrates employee achievements and contributions. Ensure that recognition is specific, timely, and aligned with employees' preferences.

3. Support Career Development:

- o   Provide opportunities for professional development and career growth. Offer training programs, mentorship, and clear pathways for advancement.

4. Promote Work/Life Balance:

- o   Implement policies that support work/life balance, such as flexible working hours, remote work options, and wellness programs.

5. Conduct Regular Engagement Assessments:

- o   Continuously monitor employee engagement through surveys, feedback mechanisms, and performance metrics. Use the data to make informed decisions and improvements.

6. Address Workload Issues:

- o   Regularly review and adjust workloads to ensure they are manageable. Provide resources and support to help employees manage their responsibilities effectively.

Employee engagement is a multifaceted aspect of organizational health that requires ongoing attention and evaluation. By focusing on effective work organization, job security, recognition, career advancement, workload management, and work/life balance, organizations can foster a highly engaged and motivated workforce. Regular assessment and proactive improvements in these areas will enhance overall employee satisfaction, productivity, and retention, contributing to long-term organizational success.

Knowledge accessibility

Enhancing Knowledge Accessibility: Key Strategies and Considerations

Knowledge accessibility is essential for optimizing organizational performance and employee effectiveness. It involves ensuring that job-related information, training, and best practices are readily available to employees, promoting effective teamwork, and using efficient collection systems. Here's how to ensure that knowledge is accessible and effectively utilized within an organization.

Key Factors for Improving Knowledge Accessibility

Availability of Job-Related Information and Training

Assessment Criteria:

- Information Access: Evaluate whether job-related information is easily accessible to employees. This includes having up-to-date manuals, guidelines, and resources that are readily available.
- Training Resources: Assess the availability and accessibility of training programs that are necessary for employees to perform their roles effectively. This includes both initial training and ongoing development opportunities.

Monitoring Methods:

- Surveys and Feedback: Conduct surveys or interviews to understand employees' perceptions of how accessible job-related information and training resources are. Collect feedback on any barriers they encounter in accessing these resources.
- Resource Audit: Perform an audit of the available training materials and information systems to ensure they are current, comprehensive, and accessible.

Encouragement and Facilitation of Teamwork

Assessment Criteria:

- Team Collaboration: Determine how well teamwork is encouraged and facilitated within the organization. Effective teamwork should be supported through collaborative tools, team-building activities, and a culture that values cooperation.

- Communication Channels: Evaluate the availability and effectiveness of communication channels that enable team members to collaborate easily.

Monitoring Methods:

- Team Surveys: Use surveys to assess team members' experiences with teamwork and collaboration. Measure the effectiveness of tools and practices that support teamwork.
- Collaboration Tools Review: Review the tools and platforms used for collaboration (e.g., project management software, communication tools) to ensure they meet the needs of the teams.

Sharing and Improving Best Practices

Assessment Criteria:

- Best Practices Sharing: Assess how well best practices are shared across the organization. This includes formal mechanisms for disseminating knowledge, such as workshops, newsletters, or internal knowledge bases.
- Continuous Improvement: Evaluate the processes in place for improving best practices based on feedback and new insights. Organizations should have mechanisms for updating and refining best practices regularly.

Monitoring Methods:

- Knowledge Sharing Metrics: Track the frequency and effectiveness of best practice sharing through metrics such as the number of shared practices, participation rates in knowledge-sharing sessions, and feedback from employees.

- Improvement Reviews: Review how best practices are updated and refined over time. Analyze the processes for incorporating feedback and making improvements.

Efficient Collection Systems

Assessment Criteria:

- Information Collection: Evaluate the systems used to collect and store information. Effective collection systems should ensure that information is captured accurately and is easily retrievable.
- Ease of Access: Assess how easily employees can access the collected information. This includes having user-friendly interfaces and search functionalities that allow quick retrieval of relevant data.

Monitoring Methods:

- System Usability Reviews: Conduct reviews of the information collection systems to assess their usability and effectiveness. Gather feedback from users on their experience with accessing and retrieving information.
- Data Access Analysis: Analyze how often and how effectively employees access the collected information. Identify any issues or barriers that may hinder easy access.

Strategies for Enhancing Knowledge Accessibility

1. Implement User-Friendly Knowledge Management Systems:

    o Invest in knowledge management systems that are intuitive and user-friendly. Ensure that these systems support easy retrieval of information and facilitate collaboration.

2. Promote a Knowledge-Sharing Culture:

    o Foster a culture that values knowledge sharing and collaboration. Encourage employees to share their expertise and learn from each other through regular meetings, workshops, and internal forums.

3. Regularly Update Training Materials and Resources:

- Ensure that training materials and job-related information are regularly updated to reflect current practices and knowledge. Provide ongoing training opportunities to keep employees informed and skilled.

4. Leverage Technology for Collaboration:

- Use collaborative tools and platforms to support teamwork. Implement project management software, communication tools, and other technologies that enhance collaboration and information sharing.

5. Facilitate Continuous Improvement:

- Establish processes for reviewing and improving best practices. Encourage employees to provide feedback and suggest improvements to existing practices.

6. Monitor and Evaluate Knowledge Accessibility:

- Continuously monitor the effectiveness of knowledge accessibility initiatives. Use feedback, surveys, and performance metrics to identify areas for improvement and make necessary adjustments.

Effective knowledge accessibility is critical for enhancing organizational performance and employee productivity. By ensuring that job-related information and training are readily available, encouraging and facilitating teamwork, sharing and improving best practices, and using efficient collection systems, organizations can create a more informed, collaborative, and agile workforce. Implementing these strategies will help in optimizing knowledge management processes and supporting the overall success of the organization.

Workforce optimization

Optimizing Workforce Performance: Essential Strategies and Considerations

Workforce optimization involves aligning processes, training, working conditions, performance management, and hiring practices to maximize employee productivity and organizational effectiveness. Implementing a comprehensive approach to workforce optimization ensures that employees are well-supported, performance standards are clear, and the right talent is in place. Here's how to achieve effective workforce optimization through key practices:

Key Factors for Workforce Optimization

Well-Defined Work Processes and Effective Training

Assessment Criteria:

- Process Clarity: Evaluate whether work processes are clearly defined and documented. This includes having standardized procedures and workflows that employees can follow.
- Training Effectiveness: Assess the quality and impact of training programs. Training should be relevant, comprehensive, and aligned with job requirements to ensure employees are well-prepared to perform their roles effectively.

Monitoring Methods:

- Process Reviews: Conduct regular reviews of work processes to ensure they are well-defined and up-to-date. Solicit feedback from employees on process clarity and areas for improvement.
- Training Evaluations: Use feedback surveys and performance assessments to evaluate the effectiveness of training programs. Track how well training translates into improved job performance and skill application.

Supportive Working Conditions

Assessment Criteria:

- Work Environment: Assess whether the working conditions are conducive to high performance. This includes evaluating the physical workspace, access to necessary resources, and overall work environment.
- Employee Well-being: Evaluate the support provided for employee well-being, including health and safety measures, work-life balance initiatives, and ergonomics.

Monitoring Methods:

- Workplace Surveys: Conduct surveys to gather employee feedback on working conditions and overall satisfaction with their work environment.
- Workplace Audits: Perform regular audits of the physical workspace and support systems to ensure they meet high standards and support employee productivity.

High-Performance Expectations and Rewards

Assessment Criteria:

- Performance Expectations: Evaluate the clarity and communication of performance expectations. Employees should have a clear understanding of what is expected of them and how performance will be measured.
- Reward Systems: Assess the effectiveness of reward systems in recognizing and incentivizing high performance. Rewards should be aligned with performance outcomes and be meaningful to employees.

Monitoring Methods:

- Performance Reviews: Use performance review data to assess whether high performance is consistently recognized and rewarded. Analyze the correlation between performance and rewards.
- Reward Program Effectiveness: Gather feedback from employees on the perceived fairness and impact of reward systems. Track the success of reward programs in motivating high performance.

Skill-Based Hiring and Thorough Orientation

Assessment Criteria:

- Hiring Practices: Evaluate whether hiring decisions are based on the skills and qualifications necessary for the role. Ensure that the recruitment process effectively assesses candidate skills and fit.
- Orientation Programs: Assess the thoroughness of orientation programs for new hires. Orientation should provide comprehensive information about the organization, role expectations, and resources available.

Monitoring Methods:

- Hiring Metrics: Analyze recruitment data to ensure that hires are selected based on their skills and qualifications. Review the effectiveness of selection processes and their impact on job performance.
- Orientation Feedback: Collect feedback from new hires about their orientation experience. Evaluate the effectiveness of orientation in helping new employees integrate into their roles and the organization.

Effective Employee Performance Management Systems

Assessment Criteria:

- Performance Management: Evaluate the effectiveness of performance management systems in setting objectives, providing feedback, and measuring performance. Systems should support continuous improvement and development.
- Feedback Mechanisms: Assess how feedback is provided to employees and how performance issues are addressed. Effective feedback should be constructive, timely, and supportive.

Monitoring Methods:

- Performance Management Reviews: Review the performance management process to ensure it is effective and aligns with organizational goals. Analyze performance data to identify trends and areas for improvement.
- Feedback Surveys: Conduct surveys to gather employee feedback on the performance management system. Assess the perceived fairness and effectiveness of feedback and performance evaluations.

Strategies for Optimizing Workforce Performance

Define and Document Work Processes:

- Clearly define and document work processes to ensure consistency and efficiency. Regularly review and update processes to adapt to changes and improve performance.

Invest in Effective Training Programs:

- Develop and implement training programs that are relevant and effective. Use feedback and performance data to continually improve training content and delivery.

Enhance Working Conditions:

- Create a supportive work environment that fosters high performance. Address physical workspace needs, provide necessary resources, and support employee well-being.

Implement Strong Performance Management Systems:

- Develop a robust performance management system that includes clear expectations, regular feedback, and opportunities for development. Ensure that performance management practices are fair and transparent.

Focus on Skill-Based Hiring:

- Prioritize skill-based hiring to ensure that new hires have the necessary competencies for their roles. Provide thorough orientation programs to help new employees integrate effectively.

Recognize and Reward High Performance:

- Establish reward systems that recognize and incentivize high performance. Ensure that rewards are aligned with performance outcomes and are meaningful to employees.

Optimizing workforce performance requires a multifaceted approach that includes defining clear work processes, providing effective training, creating supportive working conditions, implementing skill-based hiring practices, and managing performance effectively. By focusing on these key areas, organizations can enhance employee productivity, satisfaction, and overall effectiveness, leading to greater success and achievement of organizational goals.

Learning capacity

Enhancing Learning Capacity: Key Strategies and Considerations

Learning capacity is vital for fostering continuous improvement and innovation within an organization. It involves creating an environment where new ideas are welcomed, training is effective, career development is supported, leadership values learning, and technology aids in training management. Here's how to optimize learning capacity across these critical areas:

Key Factors for Enhancing Learning Capacity

Welcoming New Ideas

Assessment Criteria:

- Idea Acceptance: Evaluate whether the organization actively encourages and values new ideas from employees. This includes having mechanisms for submitting and discussing new ideas.
- Feedback Mechanisms: Assess how feedback on new ideas is provided and how it influences decision-making and implementation.

Monitoring Methods:

- Employee Surveys: Conduct surveys to gauge employees' perceptions of how welcoming the organization is to new ideas and whether they feel their suggestions are valued.
- Idea Implementation Tracking: Track the number of new ideas submitted and implemented, and analyze the impact of these ideas on organizational performance.

Practical and Goal-Oriented Training

Assessment Criteria:

- Training Relevance: Evaluate whether training programs are practical and aligned with the organization's goals. Training should address real job challenges and support strategic objectives.

- Training Effectiveness: Assess the impact of training on employee performance and organizational outcomes. Ensure that training content is applicable and useful.

Monitoring Methods:

- Training Evaluations: Use feedback forms and assessments to evaluate the relevance and effectiveness of training programs. Collect data on how training supports organizational goals and improves job performance.
- Performance Metrics: Analyze performance metrics to determine the impact of training on achieving organizational objectives and improving employee skills.

Formal Career Development Plans

Assessment Criteria:

- Development Planning: Assess whether employees have access to formal career development plans that outline their growth opportunities and career paths within the organization.
- Career Support: Evaluate the support provided to employees in developing and following their career plans, including mentoring and coaching.

Monitoring Methods:

- Career Plan Reviews: Review career development plans to ensure they are formalized and tailored to individual employees' goals and aspirations.
- Employee Feedback: Collect feedback from employees on the effectiveness of career development support and opportunities for advancement.

Leadership Valuing Learning

Assessment Criteria:

- Leadership Support: Evaluate how leaders demonstrate the value of learning and professional development. This includes setting examples, supporting learning initiatives, and encouraging continuous improvement.
- Visible Commitment: Assess whether leadership visibly supports and prioritizes learning through actions and communication.

Monitoring Methods:

- Leadership Surveys: Conduct surveys or interviews with employees to gauge their perceptions of leadership's commitment to learning and development.
- Observation: Observe leadership behavior and communication regarding learning and development initiatives to assess the level of support and emphasis placed on these activities.

Automation Through Learning Management Systems (LMS)

Assessment Criteria:

- System Functionality: Evaluate the functionality of the Learning Management System (LMS) in automating training processes, such as scheduling, tracking, and reporting.
- User Experience: Assess how user-friendly the LMS is for employees and administrators. Ensure that the system supports easy access to training resources and tracks progress effectively.

Monitoring Methods:

- LMS Performance Reviews: Review the performance and effectiveness of the LMS, including its ability to automate and streamline training processes. Collect feedback from users on system usability and functionality.

- Data Analysis: Analyze data from the LMS to evaluate its impact on training efficiency, employee engagement, and overall learning outcomes.

Strategies for Enhancing Learning Capacity

Foster an Innovative Culture:

- Create an environment that encourages and rewards new ideas. Implement mechanisms for employees to submit and discuss their ideas, and recognize contributions that lead to positive changes.

Align Training with Organizational Goals:

- Design training programs that are practical and directly support the organization's strategic objectives. Ensure that training content is relevant to job roles and addresses key organizational challenges.

Develop Formal Career Plans:

- Establish formal career development plans for employees, outlining potential growth paths and opportunities. Provide support through mentoring, coaching, and resources to help employees achieve their career goals.

Demonstrate Leadership Commitment to Learning:

- Ensure that leaders actively support and prioritize learning initiatives. Encourage leaders to model a commitment to continuous development and to actively engage in learning opportunities themselves.

Leverage Learning Management Systems:

- Implement an effective LMS to automate and streamline training processes. Use the system to track progress, provide access to resources, and generate reports that support learning and development efforts.

Enhancing learning capacity requires a comprehensive approach that includes welcoming new ideas, providing practical training, supporting career development, demonstrating leadership commitment, and utilizing technology effectively. By focusing on these key areas, organizations can create a learning-centric environment that drives continuous improvement, supports employee growth, and aligns with organizational goals. Implementing these strategies will help foster a culture of learning and development, ultimately contributing to organizational success and employee satisfaction.

CHAPTER 6

TALENT ACQUISITION

Question

Introduction

The journey of building a successful team begins with hiring the right people. Effective hiring practices are crucial as they lay the foundation for future performance and organizational culture. At the core of a successful hiring process is the interviewing stage, where the selection of candidates is critical. This book advocates for behavioral interviewing as a key method for assessing candidates.

Behavioral Interviewing: An Overview

Behavioral interviewing is a systematic approach that focuses on evaluating candidates based on their past behaviors and experiences. Unlike traditional interviewing techniques that might rely on hypothetical questions or theoretical discussions, behavioral interviewing delves into concrete examples from a candidate's past. This method aims to uncover how a candidate has demonstrated specific behaviors, skills, and abilities in previous roles, providing insight into their potential to excel in similar situations within your organization.

Why Behavioral Interviewing?

1. Evidence-Based Assessment: Behavioral interviewing is rooted in the premise that past behavior is the best predictor of future performance. By asking candidates to provide examples of how

they handled various situations in the past, you can gain a clearer picture of their actual capabilities and problem-solving skills. This approach moves beyond general impressions and focuses on concrete evidence of performance.

2. Consistency and Objectivity: This interviewing method ensures a consistent and objective evaluation of all candidates. By using standardized questions that explore specific competencies and experiences, you minimize biases and subjectivity in the selection process. This leads to a fairer comparison among candidates and helps in making more informed hiring decisions.

3. Real-World Relevance: Behavioral interviews are designed to mirror the real-world scenarios candidates are likely to face in the role they are applying for. This makes the interview process more relevant and allows you to assess how candidates might perform in actual job situations. It also helps in identifying candidates who are not only skilled but also fit well with the organizational culture and values.

The Behavioral Interviewing Process

1. Identify Key Competencies: Before conducting interviews, define the key competencies, skills, and behaviors required for the role. These might include problem-solving abilities, teamwork, leadership, communication skills, and other relevant traits. This ensures that the interview questions are aligned with the needs of the role and the organization.

2. Develop Structured Questions: Create a set of structured questions that prompt candidates to provide specific examples of how they have demonstrated the identified competencies in the past. For instance, instead of asking, "How would you handle a difficult team member?" you might ask, "Can you describe a time when you successfully managed a challenging team member? What actions did you take, and what was the outcome?"

3. Use the STAR Technique: Encourage candidates to answer questions using the STAR technique—Situation, Task, Action, Result. This method helps candidates provide clear and detailed responses by breaking down their experiences into four parts:

   o Situation: Describe the context or background of the experience.
   o Task: Explain the specific task or challenge faced.
   o Action: Detail the actions taken to address the situation.
   o Result: Share the outcome or results achieved.

4. Evaluate Responses: Assess candidates' responses based on how well they demonstrate the desired competencies and skills. Look for concrete examples and evidence of successful outcomes. Consider how their past behavior aligns with the requirements of the role and the organizational culture.

5. Ensure a Balanced Perspective: While behavioral interviewing focuses on past experiences, it's also important to consider other factors such as cultural fit, enthusiasm for the role, and alignment with the organization's values. Combine insights from behavioral interviews with other assessment methods to make well-rounded hiring decisions.

Best Practices for Behavioral Interviewing

1. Prepare Thoroughly: Prepare for interviews by reviewing the job description, competencies, and candidate resumes. Develop a clear set of questions and scenarios to explore each candidate's qualifications thoroughly.

2. Create a Comfortable Environment: Set a positive and welcoming tone during the interview to help candidates feel at ease. This can lead to more genuine responses and a better assessment of their true abilities.

3. Train Interviewers: Ensure that all interviewers are trained in behavioral interviewing techniques and understand how

to evaluate responses consistently. This helps in maintaining fairness and accuracy in the assessment process.

4. Document Responses: Take detailed notes during the interview to capture the candidate's responses accurately. This documentation is crucial for making informed decisions and providing feedback if needed.

5. Review and Reflect: After the interview, review the candidate's responses and reflect on their potential fit for the role and the organization. Discuss impressions and evaluations with other interviewers to reach a consensus.

Behavioral interviewing is a powerful tool for building a successful team. By focusing on past behaviors and concrete examples, you gain valuable insights into a candidate's suitability for the role and their potential for success within your organization. Implementing this method effectively can enhance the hiring process, improve the quality of hires, and contribute to building a high-performing team.

Behavioral interviewing

Behavioral interviewing is a structured method of interviewing. It allows you to evaluate the candidate and also compare it with other candidates.

Some examples of questions you would ask:

1. Can you tell me a little more about the situation?
2. What exactly did you do?
3. What was your specific role in this?
4. How did this turn out?
5. What other challenges did you come across? What did you do to address those?

What to look for in candidates?

We should be able to answer what knowledge, skills, abilities, and other characteristics (KSAOs) are most critical for success in this position? What behaviors are important or strategically critical for the organization?

Once you have clarity on these questions, you can then decide what competencies (i.e. clusters of KSAOs) are most strategically important to my organization when evaluating candidates.

Competency-based approach to behavioral interviewing is effective because:

1. Competencies provide direction
2. Competencies are measurable
3. Competencies can be learned
4. Competencies can distinguish and differentiate the organization
5. Competencies can integrate management practices

How to write interview questions?

One well-known approach is the STAR model. STAR – Situation, Task, Action, and Results model.

An example of how interview questions can be prepared using the STAR model:

1. Situation: What was the situation the candidate was in?
   - *"Tell me about a time..."*

2. Task: What was the task the candidate needed to accomplish?
   - *"Where you were faced with multiple competing deadlines."*

3. Action: What were the actions the candidate took to accomplish this task?
   - *"What did you do and..."*

4. Results: What were the results of these actions?
   - *"How did it turn out?"*

How to create rating scales?

Once the questions are ready you can create a rating scale, so that you can rate the candidate and then compare it with other candidates.

A generic scale would look like:

- Far exceeds requirements: Perfect answer. Demonstrates competency accurately, consistently, and independently.
- Exceeds requirements: Demonstrates competency accurately and consistently in most situations with minimal guidance.
- Meets requirements: Demonstrates competency accurately and consistently on familiar procedures and needs supervisor guidance for new skills.
- Below requirements: Demonstrates competency inconsistently, even after repeated instruction or guidance.
- Significant gap: Fails to demonstrate competency regardless of guidance provided.

Online Recruiting

Company website

A crucial part of the online hiring process is developing a company website that showcases your brand's unique personality and workplace culture. According to a recent LinkedIn survey, a company career page is the best place for employer branding.

In a highly competitive and candidate-driven job market, you want to excite people about the opportunities you offer and provide evidence that you are a values-driven, diverse, and inclusive organization.

Your website might include a dedicated recruitment page, a thought leadership blog, details about your company's core values, a diversity, equity, and inclusion statement, examples of the work you're doing to drive sustainability or support your local community, interviews with senior leaders or testimonials from employees.

Think carefully about how you choose to present this information to ensure it's attention-grabbing and memorable. If you haven't upgraded or revamped your site in a while, consider investing in the resources to do so, because first impressions matter.

Internet ad campaigns

Pay-per-click ad campaigns are a simple yet effective way to increase awareness about your organization's job openings and drive prospective candidates to your company website or recruitment page.

Social media sites, like LinkedIn, and search engines, like Google, offer pay-per-click advertising options. They can be targeted towards potential candidates from various industries or specific regions with certain skill sets. Research has found that brand awareness can be increased through Google paid ads.

Social media

Aside from pay-per-click ads, social media sites have a crucial role to play when it comes to online recruitment – and many of the features are either cheap or free to use.

Glassdoor revealed that job seekers were using social media when conducting their job search. Meanwhile, organizations are already opting to recruit via social media, finding that it's a useful way of engaging with passive job seekers.

Organizations are finding social media useful in engaging passive job seekers, according to Glassdoor and SHRM

Depending on your typical candidate demographic or the seniority of the role for which you're recruiting, sites including LinkedIn, X, Instagram, and Facebook can all be used to target candidates, market your company, and build brand awareness.

Make sure that the content you put out on social media is tailored to your target demographic and aligns with the site you are using. For example, the tone, format, and length of LinkedIn and X posts should vary significantly.

Online job sites

There are many jobs sites where you can both identify and recruit candidates (via a database of resumes) and post job openings. Take a look at sites like CareerBuilder, Monster, Indeed, Glassdoor, Google for Jobs, Craigslist, Dice, Nexxt, JobsRadar, and Jobvertise. These sites provide easy access to thousands of candidates and can help to simplify or accelerate your recruitment processes.

One of the downsides of using job boards is that you'll likely receive lots of applications from unsuitable candidates. However, specialist and targeted job boards are increasingly common and a quick Google search will help you to identify sites tailored to your specific industry and needs.

Implement pre-screening tools and skills assessments

Making a bad hire is one of the most expensive mistakes a hiring manager or recruiter can make, with the potential to cost your organization tens of thousands of dollars. Yet, according to research from CareerBuilder, employers admit they've hired the wrong person for a position.

If your organization is recruiting online, a good way to ensure you hire the right people is to implement pre-screening tools and skills assessments that can assess candidates for cultural fit, emotional intelligence (EQ), situational judgment, leadership qualities, and key skill sets, ultimately predicting their future performance at your company.

Pre-screening tools are increasingly sophisticated and affordable and, alongside reducing turnover rates, can help to identify subtle differences between similar candidates and reduce unconscious bias.

Time-to-hire is also significantly reduced as skills assessments negate the need for hiring managers and recruiters to manually screen or interview every single applicant.

Dedicated contact sourcing

Certain job boards, sites, and channels dominate the recruitment industry. They provide you with access to the biggest talent pool and are typically affordable and seamless to use. As such, it can be tempting to put all your online recruitment eggs into one basket.

But you never know when or where you might unearth your perfect candidate, which means it's much wiser to actively source candidates and advertise job openings across a range of different channels to maximize exposure. By putting in the work identifying suitable candidates within your industry or targeting specialized jobs sites you'll build out your talent pool and, in the long run, waste less time on uninterested or irrelevant parties

Online recruitment software

Online recruitment software leverages automation and artificial intelligence (AI) to take on a range of typically time-consuming and monotonous tasks to streamline your processes and enhance the overall candidate experience.

There are platforms available to screen résumés for keywords, send updates and status notifications to candidates, generate reports and analyze candidate data, post openings on your company recruitment page, schedule interviews, and keep hiring managers updated throughout the recruitment process. By automating these processes, recruiters and hiring managers can spend their time on more demanding and value-adding tasks. Meanwhile, your candidates will appreciate regular communication, transparency, and increased efficiencies.

Before investing, consider which elements of your existing recruitment processes are causing the most friction and establish your hiring priorities to determine which software will best suit your needs.

Video advertising

If one of the main disadvantages of online recruitment methods is that they are often impersonal, good use of video content promises to make the process more human.

Consider embedding videos in your job descriptions, social media posts and adverts, and throughout your website to provide prospective candidates with more intimate insights about your workplace culture. You could, for example, include interviews with current employees, video tours of your workplace, or a video of your hiring managers explaining the job role and hiring requirements. posts, or adverts than they are watching engaging and stimulating videos.

Video interviews

Video interviewing is low-effort, low-cost, and highly convenient for both employer and candidate, but it's also one of the few online recruitment methods that will help you to build a personal connection with applicants.

It's best to reserve the video interview stage of the recruitment process for shortlisted candidates so you can focus your time and effort where it really matters. In addition, always opt for structured video interviews, which means asking everyone the same questions, so you can easily compare candidates.

Another benefit of video interviews is that they can be easily recorded, allowing hiring managers or recruiters to be present and engaged during the interview, and review a candidate's responses more closely after the meeting. This also enables collaborative hiring because other team members can evaluate interview recordings. Be sure to ask a candidate's permission before recording the interview.

You could also consider integrating video content into other parts of your recruitment process. For example, once you've pre-screened candidates, you could ask them to submit a video application in replacement of a cover letter. This is a great way for you to get a better sense of their personality and accelerate the screening process.

Onboarding leaders

The HR department must take steps to integrate newly onboarded leaders into the organization. Five major tasks that leaders must undertake in their first few critical months. These are the areas in which they need the greatest integration support:

1. Assuming operational leadership: Even with the best possible exchange of information during the recruiting process, any leader in a new role (especially an outsider) will have an incomplete picture of the business— its strengths, weaknesses, opportunities, and threats. A new leader builds his or her credibility by demonstrating awareness of important operational issues, swiftly solving urgent problems, and identifying and achieving quick wins. Good early decisions on the ground have a material impact on his or her reputation as an effective leader.

2. Taking charge of the team. New leaders naturally focus on their direct reports at the outset—they know they must quickly confirm or adjust the team's composition and goals. It is often easier to decide toward the beginning whether or not to retain people, because the team's makeup is not then seen as the new leader's choice. However, this window closes soon, and focus and discipline are needed to efficiently gather information for smart decisions. It's valuable to allow a new leader to take a fresh look at the talent without coloring his or her view in advance, but it's equally valuable to share insights about individual team member's performance and development. Striking the right balance requires careful planning and coordination with HR and, typically, one or more facilitated sessions between the executive and the team during the first few weeks. The goal is to create a safe

environment for both to give timely, constructive feedback and to ask what may seem like awkward questions when relationships are just beginning to form. In this way any misperceptions about the leader's words, actions, or initial decisions can be identified and clarified before mistrust or doubt about his or her values or capabilities takes hold. Building trust early with the team enables the new leader to make key decisions with confidence that people will follow through on them.

3. Aligning with stakeholders. New leaders also need to gain the support of people over whom they have no direct authority, including their bosses, their peers, and other colleagues. Because they arrive with little or no relationship capital, they have to invest energy in building connections—and clearly signal that they know it's a priority. After identifying the most important stakeholders outside their teams, they must take time to understand their colleagues' expectations and develop a plan for how and when to connect with people. That means learning how decision-making works in the organization, who influences it, and where the centers of power reside.

4. Engaging with the culture. It's also critical to get up to speed on the values, norms, and guiding assumptions that define acceptable behavior in the new organization. Missing cues early on can negatively affect how others perceive a new leader's intentions and capabilities. The executive must also walk a fine line between working within the culture and seeking to change it.

5. Defining strategic intent. Finally, the new leader must start to shape strategy. Sometimes executives are hired for their expertise in a particular approach; other times they are chosen for their ability to develop and implement an entirely new strategy. If a new strategy is required, corresponding elements of the organization—its structure and its talent management and performance measurement processes—must be transformed to

execute it. Either way, the new leader must be clear about the path ahead.

Together these five transition tasks present a daunting challenge. Stumbles in any area can lead to serious problems or even outright derailment. Effective integration is much more likely when leaders understand—before they start in their new roles—how much progress they'll need to demonstrate in each area during the first few months. That way they can prioritize their time effectively.

CHAPTER 7

TALENT MANAGEMENT

Question

Introduction

After successfully hiring a team, the next critical step is effective talent management. Creating a great workplace and ensuring organizational effectiveness involves a range of strategic practices that support employee engagement, development, and performance. This chapter delves into how to manage your talent pool effectively, fostering an environment where employees thrive and contribute to organizational success.

Building a Great Place to Work

Cultivating a Positive Work Culture

A positive work culture is fundamental to employee satisfaction and organizational success. It encompasses shared values, beliefs, and practices that create a supportive and engaging environment. Key elements include:

- Open Communication: Foster a culture of transparency where employees feel comfortable sharing their ideas, feedback, and concerns. Regular team meetings, one-on-one discussions, and open-door policies can help achieve this.
- Recognition and Appreciation: Regularly acknowledge and reward employees' efforts and achievements. Implement

recognition programs that celebrate milestones, exceptional performance, and contributions to team success.

- Inclusivity and Diversity: Promote an inclusive environment where diverse perspectives are valued and respected. Ensure that policies and practices support diversity and provide equal opportunities for all employees.

Providing Work-Life Balance

Supporting work-life balance is essential for employee well-being and productivity. Strategies include:

- Flexible Work Arrangements: Offer options such as remote work, flexible hours, and compressed workweeks to help employees manage their personal and professional responsibilities.
- Employee Well-being Programs: Implement programs that support physical and mental health, such as wellness initiatives, counselling services, and stress management workshops.
- Encouraging Time Off: Promote the importance of taking breaks and vacations to recharge and prevent burnout. Ensure that employees feel comfortable using their leave entitlements.

Offering Career Development Opportunities

Career development opportunities are vital for retaining and motivating employees. Key practices include:

- Training and Development: Provide ongoing training programs and learning resources that help employees develop new skills and advance in their careers. This can include workshops, seminars, and online courses.
- Career Pathing: Work with employees to create clear career paths and development plans that align with their aspirations and organizational goals. Offer mentorship and coaching to support their growth.

- Promoting from Within: Whenever possible, consider internal candidates for promotions and new roles. This demonstrates a commitment to career development and helps retain top talent.

Ensuring Organizational Effectiveness

Aligning Goals and Performance

Organizational effectiveness depends on aligning individual and team goals with broader organizational objectives. Strategies include:

- Setting Clear Objectives: Develop and communicate clear, measurable goals for teams and individuals that support the organization's strategic priorities. Ensure that everyone understands how their work contributes to these objectives.
- Performance Management: Implement a robust performance management system that includes regular feedback, performance reviews, and goal-setting. Provide employees with the tools and support they need to achieve their targets.
- Monitoring Progress: Regularly review progress toward goals and adjust strategies as needed. Use performance metrics and key performance indicators (KPIs) to track success and identify areas for improvement.

Enhancing Communication and Collaboration

Effective communication and collaboration are crucial for organizational success. Practices include:

- Encouraging Teamwork: Foster a collaborative environment where teams work together to achieve common goals. Promote cross-functional projects and encourage sharing of information and resources.
- Utilizing Technology: Leverage technology to facilitate communication and collaboration. Use tools such as project

management software, collaboration platforms, and instant messaging to streamline workflows and enhance connectivity.

- Providing Feedback Channels: Establish mechanisms for employees to provide feedback on processes, practices, and organizational changes. Use this feedback to make improvements and address concerns.

Implementing Effective Leadership

Strong leadership is essential for driving organizational effectiveness. Key leadership practices include:

- Leading by Example: Leaders should model the behavior and values they expect from their teams. Demonstrate commitment to the organization's mission, embrace transparency, and uphold high ethical standards.
- Developing Leadership Skills: Invest in leadership development programs to enhance the skills of current and future leaders. Provide opportunities for leaders to receive coaching, attend training, and participate in leadership development initiatives.
- Empowering Teams: Empower leaders and managers to make decisions and take ownership of their areas. Encourage autonomy and support leaders in developing their teams and achieving their goals.

Measuring and Improving Organizational Effectiveness

- Continuous improvement is key to maintaining organizational effectiveness. Strategies include:
- Conducting Assessments: Regularly assess organizational effectiveness through employee surveys, performance reviews, and other evaluation methods. Analyze results to identify strengths and areas for improvement.
- Benchmarking: Compare organizational practices and performance against industry standards and best practices. Use

benchmarking to identify opportunities for enhancement and adopt successful strategies from other organizations.

- Implementing Action Plans: Develop and implement action plans based on assessment findings and feedback. Monitor progress and make adjustments as needed to drive continuous improvement.

Effectively managing your talent pool involves creating a positive work environment, supporting employee development, and ensuring alignment with organizational goals. By focusing on these areas, you can foster a workplace where employees feel valued, engaged, and motivated to contribute to the organization's success. Implementing these strategies will help build a strong, effective team and drive overall organizational performance.

Developing a talent pool

The following activities constitute how you can develop a talent pool:

1. Succession Planning
2. Capacity Building
3. Relationship Building
4. Bursaries
5. Internship programs
6. Apprenticeship programs
7. Connecting Talent to Value

Succession Planning

Succession planning includes:

1. Identification of key positions

   a. Current and future strategic goals and objectives
   b. Retirement forecasts
   c. Turnover rates
   d. Current and expected vacancies

    e.   Changes to existing programs and services

    f.   Highly specialized function

2. Identification of core position competencies

    a.   Reviewing job descriptions, advertisements, and relevant metric criteria

    b.   Interviewing current and former job incumbents

    c.   Interviewing supervisors, clients, and other stakeholders

    d.   Conducting focus groups or surveys

    e.   Reviewing any existing development programs (i.e., leadership competencies)

    f.   Reviewing organizational values

3. Identification of potential candidates

    a.   Circulating the expression of interest

    b.   Employees discussing career goals and objectives with their supervisor

    c.   Developing an inventory of employee skills/competencies and career interests

4. Assessment of potential candidates

    a.   Written exams

    b.   Candidate interviews

    c.   Review of resumes

    d.   Simulated work exercises

    e.   Performance reviews

    f.   Reference checks

    g.   Talent review meetings

5. Create developmental plans

    a.   Mentoring, coaching or job-shadowing

    b.   Documenting critical knowledge

    c. Exit interviews

    d. Establishing communities of practice

6. Implementation of plans

    a. How the process operates

    b. Impact of the process relative to stated objectives and goals

    c. Functional strengths and weaknesses

    d. Potential gaps in planning and assumptions

    e. Cost-effectiveness and cost-benefit

The important considerations of succession planning are:

1. What is the business case for succession planning in the organization?
2. Is planning based on short and long-term goals and objectives?
3. Have the key stakeholders and decision-makers been consulted?
4. How involved are the leaders?
5. Is succession planning linked with workforce planning?
6. Can succession planning be linked with other HR strategies?
7. Is there accountability at the department level?
8. What are the roles and responsibilities of stakeholders
9. Is the process, and its expected outcomes, clearly understood by everyone involved?
10. What decisions should be made at the department and corporate levels?
11. How will the process demonstrate value for transparency, fairness, and accessibility?
12. Is there a plan or strategy to manage employee expectations?
13. Do employees understand that they are not guaranteed a promotion?
14. How will succession planning be evaluated?
15. Do employees understand that they are responsible for managing their own career path(s)?
16. Is the work environment supportive of succession planning?

Capacity Building

The development of a team is not just for competitive advantage, but it helps build an environment for innovation and improvement. Improvement in product development and delivery of services. Leading to improvement in customer contact and satisfaction. Some of the initiatives can include:

1. Linking learning with organizational requirements of future skills (e.g., as we discussed earlier, preparing a workforce for Industry 4.0)
2. Career development
3. Reassignment/ Job Rotation
4. Training at entry-level positions

Relationship building

1. Apprentice Program
2. Internships
3. Fellowship Program
4. Part-time student employment

Bursary program

Allows selected candidates to pursue a specific area of expertise by providing candidates with the opportunity to gain valuable practical training experience in a particular field of work. The candidate, in return for the assistance, commits to work for a specified period of time.

By providing structured, on-the-job training for qualified candidates, the program can be a mutually rewarding experience, aiding trainees in their personal and professional development and helping the organization, or department, to create a more dynamic workplace and build needed skill sets for future HR planning.

Internship Program

1. Access junior professional-level workers
2. Achieve progress on projects
3. Contribute to a young person's knowledge
4. Influence a career path, by promoting your organization as a potential employer

Apprentice program

An apprentice is an opportunity for a student to learn and develop certain skills with an employer who needs to build capacity in that area. It can be viewed as an "earning while learning" arrangement.

Apprenticeships help the student gain knowledge and develop skills associated with the job and often involve:

- Supervision from experienced, seasoned professionals
- Supplemental specialized, in-class training

Connecting Talent to Value

The following framework (Figure 7) summarizes Talent Management on how to connect talent to value:

1. Goal Management: employee activities must align with the organization's business goals. And constantly monitored through continuous employee feedback (Voice of Employee), process outcomes (Voice of Process), and business outcomes (Voice of Business).
2. Compensation: Create comprehensive insight by tracking financial & business goals; and comparing target metrics to actual results to determine payouts. Motivate employees with just-in-time recognition to drive engagement and retention
3. Succession & Development: Engage and Motivate Employees with Meaningful Development Plans and Career Opportunities. Automatically match mentors & mentees to accelerate employee development.

4. Develop skills: Deliver a learning strategy that includes e-learning, classroom & virtual instructor-led training, mentoring, experiential on-the-job training, and collaboration. Complement learning with informal capabilities such as blogs, videos, multimedia playlists, Quick Guides, and documents.

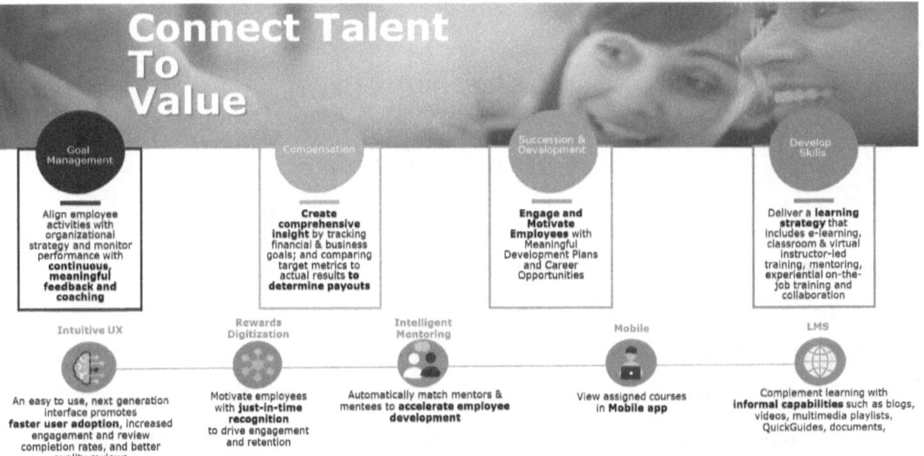

Figure 7: Talent to Value

CHAPTER 8

COMPENSATION MANAGEMENT

Question

Introduction

Compensation planning is a crucial aspect of human resources management that directly impacts employee satisfaction, motivation, and retention. A well-structured compensation plan not only attracts top talent but also aligns employee performance with organizational goals. In this chapter, we will explore the key components of employee compensation and the various methods of payout to ensure that your compensation strategy is effective and competitive.

Components of Employee Compensation

Compensation encompasses all forms of financial returns and benefits that employees receive in exchange for their work. It can be broadly categorized into several components:

Base Salary

Base salary is the fixed amount of money paid to employees on a regular basis, typically monthly or bi-weekly. It represents the primary component of compensation and is determined based on factors such as job role, level of responsibility, experience, and industry standards.

- Determining Base Salary: Base salary should be competitive with industry benchmarks and reflective of the employee's role and contributions. Regular salary reviews and adjustments based on performance, inflation, and market conditions can help maintain competitiveness.

Bonuses and Incentives

Bonuses and incentives are additional forms of compensation designed to reward employees for achieving specific performance goals or milestones. They can be categorized into:

- Performance Bonuses: Awarded based on individual or team performance. These can be tied to achieving targets, exceeding expectations, or completing key projects.
- Annual Bonuses: Often linked to the company's overall performance and profitability. Typically paid out at the end of the fiscal year or performance cycle.
- Signing Bonuses: Offered to new hires as an incentive to join the organization, especially in competitive job markets or for roles requiring specialized skills.

Commission

Commission-based compensation is common in sales and other revenue-generating roles. It is based on the amount of sales or revenue an employee generates.

- Structure: Commissions can be structured as a percentage of sales, a fixed amount per sale, or a tiered system where higher performance yields higher commission rates. Clear communication about commission structures and targets is essential for motivation and transparency.

Profit Sharing

Profit sharing involves distributing a portion of the company's profits among employees. It is designed to align employees' interests with the company's financial success.

- Types of Profit Sharing: Profit sharing can be structured as cash bonuses, contributions to retirement plans, or other financial benefits. The distribution method and criteria should be clearly defined and communicated to employees.

Stock Options and Equity

Stock options and equity grants provide employees with ownership stakes in the company. This can be an attractive component of compensation, especially in startups and high-growth organizations.

- Stock Options: Allow employees to purchase company stock at a predetermined price, often referred to as the exercise price. Vesting schedules typically determine when employees can exercise their options.
- Equity Grants: Provide employees with shares or equity units in the company, which may be subject to vesting conditions and other terms.

Benefits

- Employee benefits are non-wage compensations that contribute to overall job satisfaction and well-being. They can include:
- Health Insurance: Coverage for medical, dental, and vision care.
- Retirement Plans: Employer contributions to retirement savings plans, such as 401(k) or pension plans.
- Paid Time Off (PTO): Vacation days, sick leave, and personal days.
- Other Benefits: Life insurance, disability coverage, employee assistance programs, and wellness initiatives.

Methods of Payout

- The payout methods for compensation components vary based on the nature of the compensation and organizational practices. Here's a look at common payout methods:

Direct Deposit

- Direct deposit is the most common method for paying base salary and bonuses. It involves electronically transferring funds from the employer's account to the employee's bank account on a scheduled basis.

Advantages: Direct deposit is secure, convenient, and ensures timely payments. It reduces administrative overhead and eliminates the risk of lost or stolen checks.

Payroll Checks

- Payroll checks are less common today but are still used by some organizations, especially where direct deposit is not feasible.

Considerations: Payroll checks should be managed carefully to ensure timely delivery and avoid issues related to lost or stolen checks.

Commission and Bonus Payments

- Commission and bonus payments are typically processed separately from regular salary payments. They may be paid on a monthly, quarterly, or annual basis, depending on the organization's compensation structure.

Timing: Clearly define the timing and conditions for commission and bonus payments to ensure transparency and manage expectations.

Stock Options and Equity Grants

- Stock options and equity grants have specific vesting schedules and exercise terms. The payout or benefit realization depends on the company's stock performance and the employee's vesting period.

Administration: Proper administration and communication about stock options and equity grants are crucial for managing employee expectations and ensuring compliance with regulatory requirements.

Benefits Enrolment and Administration

- Benefits are usually managed through separate enrolment processes and administered by third-party providers or in-house HR teams. Employees typically choose their benefits during open enrolment periods.
- Communication: Ensure that employees understand their benefits options and how to enrol or make changes. Provide clear information about coverage, costs, and how to access benefits.

Effective compensation planning involves understanding and strategically managing the various components of employee pay and benefits. By offering a well-rounded compensation package that includes base salary, bonuses, commissions, equity, and benefits, you can attract and retain top talent, drive performance, and enhance employee satisfaction. Implementing clear and transparent payout methods further ensures that your compensation strategy supports organizational goals and fosters a positive work environment.

Principles of compensation

1. Differences in pay should be based on differences in job requirements.
2. Wage & salary levels should align with those prevailing in the job market.
3. Follow the principle of equal pay for equal work.
4. Recognize individual differences in ability & contributions.
5. The employees & trade unions should be involved in establishing wage rates.
6. The wages should be sufficient to ensure the worker & his family a reasonable standard of living.

Components of Compensation

Direct Compensation

1. Medical Reimbursement
2. Special Allowance
3. Bonus
4. Leave Travel Allowance
5. Conveyance
6. House Rent Allowance
7. Basic Salary

Indirect Compensation

1. Overtime Policy
2. Hospitalization
3. Insurance
4. Leave Travel
5. Retirement Benefits
6. Holiday Homes
7. Flexible Timings
8. Leave Policy

Basic wages

Basic wages / salaries refer to the cash component of the wage structure based on which other elements of compensation may be structured. It is normally a fixed amount which is subject to changes based on annual increments or subject to periodical pay hikes. Wages represent hourly rates of pay, and salary refers to the monthly rate of pay, irrespective of the number of hours put in by the employee. Wages and salaries are subject to the annual increments. They differ from employee to employee, and depend upon the nature of job, seniority, and merit.

Dearness allowance

The payment of dearness allowance facilitates employees and workers to face the price increase or inflation of prices of goods and services consumed by him. The onslaught of price increase has a major bearing on the living conditions of the labour.

The increasing prices reduce the compensation to nothing and the money's worth is coming down based on the level of inflation. The payment of dearness allowance, which may be a fixed percentage on the basic wage, enables the employees to face the increasing prices.

Incentives

Incentives are paid in addition to wages and salaries and are also called 'payments by results'. Incentives depend upon productivity, sales, profit, or cost reduction efforts. There are:

1.   Individual incentive schemes, and
2.   Group incentive programs.

Bonus

The bonus can be paid in different ways. It can be fixed percentage on the basic wage paid annually or in proportion to the profitability. The Government also prescribes a minimum statutory bonus for all employees and workers. There is also a bonus plan which compensates the managers and employees based on the sales revenue or profit margin achieved. Bonus plans can also be based on piece wages but depends upon the productivity of labour.

Non-monetary benefits

These benefits give psychological satisfaction to employees even when financial benefit is not available. Such benefits are:

1.   Recognition of merit through certificate, etc.
2.   Offering challenging job responsibilities

3. Promoting growth prospects,
4. Comfortable working conditions,
5. Competent supervision, and
6. Job sharing and flexi-time.

Commissions

Commission to managers and employees may be based on the sales revenue or profits of the company. It is always a fixed percentage on the target achieved. For taxation purposes, commission is again a taxable component of compensation.

The payment of commission as a component of commission is practiced heavily on target based sales. Depending upon the targets achieved, companies may pay a commission on a monthly or periodical basis.

Fringe benefits

Fringe benefits may be defined as wide range of benefits and services that employees receive as an integral part of their total compensation package. They are based on critical job factors and performance. Fringe benefits constitute indirect compensation as they are usually extended as a condition of employment and not directly related to performance of concerned employee. They include benefits such as paid vacation, pension, health and insurance plans, etc. Such benefits are computable in terms of money and the amount of benefit is generally not predetermined. The purpose of fringe benefits is to retain efficient and capable people in the organization over a long period. They foster loyalty and acts as a security base for the employees.

Profit sharing

Profit-sharing is regarded as a stepping stone to industrial democracy. Profit-sharing is an agreement by which employees receive a share, fixed in advance of the profits. Profit-sharing usually involves the determination of an organization's profit at the end of the fiscal year and the distribution of a percentage of the profits to the workers qualified to share in the earnings.

Factors in deciding the compensation

External factors

1. Compliance with the law of the land
2. Demand and Supply of labor
3. Cost of living
4. Government
5. Prevailing wage rates
6. Labor union and collective bargaining

Internal factors

1. Capacity to pay
2. Top management philosophy
3. Job requirements
4. Organizational politics
5. Employee-related factors
6. Productivity of workers
7. Job requirements

Wage and salary surveys

A wage and salary survey is used to compile market pay data for a plethora of jobs on either a local or nationwide basis. This survey is usually performed in order to assess the effectiveness of a company's current pay structure and practices.

Surveys are used to plan future methods of compensation, and they can be instrumental in exposing gaps and waste stemming from current policies and procedures.

A comprehensive survey may also provide companies with wage data from other companies –this will allow them to assess their own compensatory policies and adjust them accordingly.

Survey data is compiled using various data and records from human resource departments. Information will usually be displayed on a wage curve.

Wage Curve

Wage curve, in simple terms, summarises the fact that a worker who is already employed in an area where the unemployment rate is high earns far less compared to an area or a region in the country where there are fewer jobs available. Labour supply is a function of wage rate.

The wage curve is a graphical representation of unemployment levels and wages are mapped on a graph when presented in local terms or for a specific region. It is seen that there is a negative relationship between the levels of unemployment and wages.

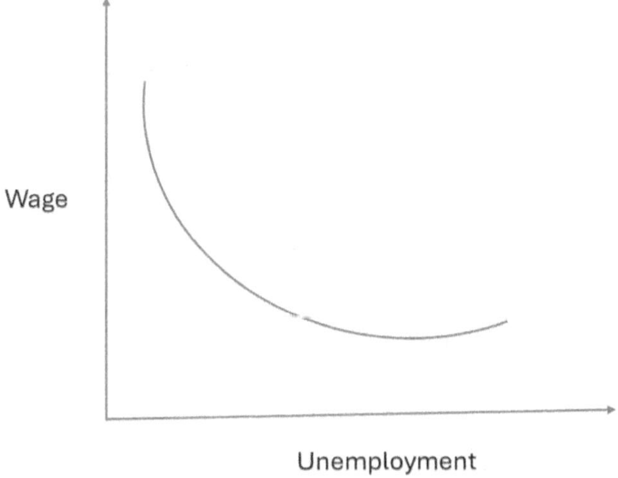

Figure 8: The wage curve

Variable pay

Variable pay systems	Service pay systems
Some jobs contribute more to the organization than others	Time spent is the primary measure of employee contribution
Some people perform better than others	Length of service is the primary differentiating factor among people

Variable pay systems	Service pay systems
Employees who perform better should receive more compensation	Contributions are recognized through different amounts of base pay
A portion of some employees' total compensation should be contingent on performance	Apportioning rewards based on individual performance is considered to be divisive.

Types of Variable Pay Plans

Individual

1. Piece rate
2. Sales commissions
3. Bonuses
4. Special recognitions (trips, merchandise)
5. Safety awards
6. Attendance bonuses

Group/Team

1. Gainsharing
2. Quality improvement
3. Cost reduction

Organization-wide

1. Profit sharing
2. Employee stock options
3. Executive stock options
4. Deferred compensation

International compensation management

Base salary

Expatriate salaries typically are set according to the base pay of the home countries. The salaries usually are paid in Home currency, local currency, or a combination of the two. The base pay also serves as the benchmarks against which bonuses and benefits are calculated.

Benefits

Benefits constitute a substantial portion of international compensation (approx. one third of compensation for regular employees is benefits). Basically an employee tends to join and stay with an organization which guarantees an attractive benefits programme. Vacation along with holidays and rest breaks help employees mitigate fatigue and enhance productivity during the hours employees actually work.

Allowance

The most common allowance relates to the cost of living–an adjustment for differences in the cost of living between the home country and foreign country assignment. This allowance is designed to provide the expatriate with the same standard of living that he or she enjoyed in the home country. Spouse assistance, housing allowance, home leave allowance, relocation allowance, and educational allowance are popular in expats compensation. These allowances are often contingent upon tax–equalization policies and practices in both the home and the host countries.

Incentives

An additional payment (or other remuneration) to employees as a means of increasing output. Increasingly, MNCs these days are designing special incentive programmes for keeping expatriates motivated. In the process, a growing number of firms have dropped the ongoing premium for overseas assignments and replaced it with a one–time, lump-sum premium. The lump–sum payment has at least three advantages:

1. First, expatriates realize that they are paid this only once and that too when they accept an overseas assignment. So the payment tends to retain its motivational value.
2. Second: costs to the company are less because there is only one payment and no future financial commitment
3. Third, less chances for premature repatriation.

Long-term benefits

The most common long-term benefits offered to employees of MNCs are Employee Stock Option Schemes (ESOS). Traditionally E-SOS were used as means to reward top management or key people of the MNCs. Some of the commonly used stock option schemes are:

1. Employee Stock Option Plan (ESOP): a certain number of shares are reserved for purchase and issuance to key employees. Such shares serve as incentive for employees to build long-term value for the company.
2. Restricted Stock Unit (RSU): This is a plan established by a company, where in units of stocks are provided with restrictions on when they can be exercised. It is usually issued as partial compensation for employees. The restrictions generally lifts in 3-5 years when the stock vests
3. Employee Stock Purchase Plan (ESPP): This is a plan wherein the company sells shares to its employees usually, at a discount.

Importantly, the company deducts the purchase price of these shares every month from the employee's salary.

A closer look at total rewards

Total Rewards Strategy	Definition
Compensation	
Base pay	Wages and salaries
Merit pay	Base-pay increases based on employee performance
Incentives	Cash bonuses based on employee performance
Total Rewards Strategy	**Definition**
Promotions	Base-pay increases based on potential to perform new job
Pay increases	Base-pay increases based on length of service with the organization
Benefits	
Health and welfare	Payment for injuries and illness both on and off the job
Paid time off	Payment for vacation time or excused days from work
Retirement	Payment for work no longer performed based on length of employment
Personal Growth	
Training	Skill development through on – or off-the-job instruction
Career development	On-the-job coaching to develop skills
Performance management	Ongoing goal setting and feedback to develop skills

Table 3: Total Rewards

CHAPTER 9

HR TECHNOLOGY

Question

Introduction

In today's experience economy, where the focus is not just on data but on the holistic employee experience, technology plays a pivotal role in transforming HR functions and driving employee engagement. This shift is marked by a transition from traditional HR technology to what is now known as Work Technology. This chapter explores how technology enables, automates, and enhances HR functions, and how it contributes to creating a superior employee experience.

The Experience Economy and HR Technology

Understanding the Experience Economy

The experience economy emphasizes creating meaningful and engaging experiences for employees, beyond just transactional interactions. In this context, employee experience encompasses every touchpoint an employee encounters during their tenure with an organization—from recruitment and onboarding to performance management and career development.

The Shift from HR Technology to Work Technology

Traditional HR technology typically focuses on automating and managing HR processes such as payroll, benefits administration, and recruitment. However, the evolution towards Work Technology involves a broader, more integrated approach that encompasses tools designed to enhance the overall work experience, improve collaboration, and foster a more engaging workplace environment.

Key Areas of Impact

- Employee Experience Platforms (EXP): These platforms aggregate various HR functions, providing a unified interface that enhances employee interaction with HR services. They often include features such as self-service portals, personalized dashboards, and integrated feedback systems.
- Integrated Systems: Modern Work Technology integrates with other enterprise systems such as ERP (Enterprise Resource Planning) and CRM (Customer Relationship Management), providing a seamless flow of information and a more cohesive experience for employees.

Technology in Enabling and Automating HR Functions

Recruitment and Onboarding

- Applicant Tracking Systems (ATS): Automate the recruitment process by managing job postings, tracking applicants, and facilitating communication. They help streamline the hiring process and ensure that the best candidates are selected efficiently.
- Onboarding Platforms: Offer digital onboarding solutions that provide new hires with all necessary information and training materials. These platforms can automate the completion of forms, schedule training sessions, and facilitate introductions to team members.

Performance Management

- Performance Management Systems: Automate performance reviews, goal setting, and feedback processes. These systems often include features for setting objectives, tracking progress, and conducting evaluations, ensuring that performance management is continuous and data-driven.

- 360-Degree Feedback Tools: Enable comprehensive performance assessments by collecting feedback from various stakeholders, including peers, subordinates, and supervisors. This technology provides a well-rounded view of employee performance and areas for development.

Learning and Development

- Learning Management Systems (LMS): Facilitate the delivery of training and development programs. They support various learning formats, including e-learning, virtual classrooms, and mobile learning, and track employee progress and completion.
- Personalized Learning Paths: Utilize AI and data analytics to create customized learning and development plans based on individual needs, career aspirations, and performance gaps.

Employee Engagement

- Employee Feedback Tools: Collect real-time feedback through surveys, polls, and suggestion boxes. These tools help organizations gauge employee sentiment and address concerns promptly.
- Recognition Platforms: Automate and streamline employee recognition programs, allowing peers and managers to acknowledge contributions and achievements in a timely and impactful manner.

Technology Driving Employee Experience

Enhancing Communication and Collaboration

- Unified Communication Tools: Integrate chat, video conferencing, and project management tools to facilitate seamless communication and collaboration among employees, regardless of location.
- Collaborative Workspaces: Use digital platforms to create virtual workspaces where teams can collaborate on projects, share documents, and track progress in real-time.

Personalization and Employee Self-Service

- Personalized Dashboards: Provide employees with personalized access to HR services, such as benefits enrolment, payroll information, and career development resources.
- Self-Service Portals: Empower employees to manage their own HR-related tasks, such as updating personal information, requesting time off, and accessing training materials.

Data-Driven Insights and Analytics

- People Analytics: Utilize advanced analytics to gain insights into employee behavior, performance trends, and engagement levels. This data can inform decision-making and help tailor HR strategies to better meet employee needs.
- Predictive Analytics: Leverage predictive modeling to anticipate future HR needs, such as turnover rates and talent gaps, and proactively address potential issues.

Well-being and Work-Life Balance

- Employee Well-being Platforms: Offer tools and resources to support employee mental and physical health, such as wellness programs, counselling services, and stress management resources.
- Work-Life Integration Tools: Provide technology solutions that support flexible working arrangements, such as remote work and

flexible scheduling, to help employees achieve a better work-life balance.

In the experience economy, technology plays a critical role in shaping the employee experience and enhancing HR functions. By embracing Work Technology, organizations can create a more engaging, efficient, and supportive work environment. The integration of advanced HR tools and platforms facilitates seamless processes, drives employee engagement, and ultimately contributes to organizational success. As technology continues to evolve, staying ahead of trends and leveraging new innovations will be key to maintaining a competitive edge and fostering a positive employee experience.

HR Technology to Work Technology

This means that everything we now buy must feel useful and important as a tool for getting work done.

HR Technology

1. HRMS
2. Payroll
3. Recruiting
4. Benefits
5. Goals
6. Recognition
7. Learning
8. Opportunities
9. Pay
10. Engagement
11. Surveys
12. Feedback
13. Development
14. Career

Work Technology

1. Wellbeing
2. Family
3. Career
4. Lifestyle
5. Health
6. Email
7. Video
8. Chat
9. Documents
10. Processes
11. Goals
12. Recognition
13. Learning
14. Opportunities
15. Pay
16. Finance
17. Family
18. Photos
19. Events
20. Fitness
21. Neighbors
22. House
23. Feelings
24. Transitions

Evolution of HR Functions to Work Technology

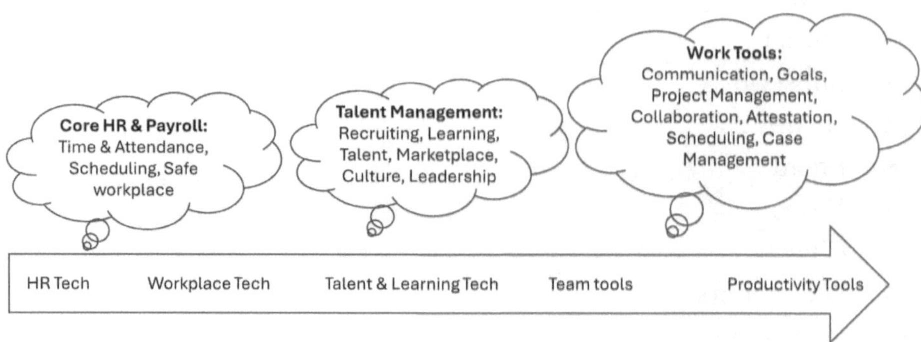

Figure 9: Evolution of HR Functions to Work Tech

HR Tech Architecture

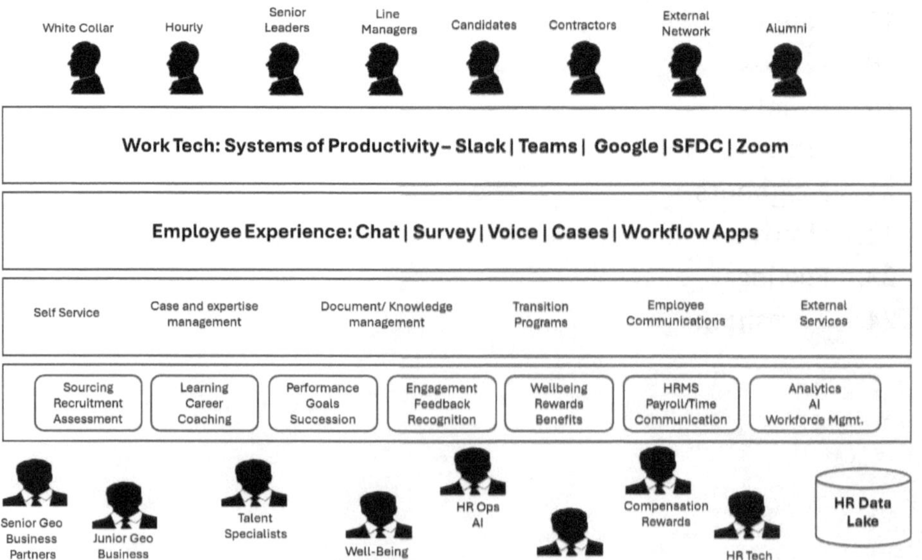

Figure 10: HR Tech Architecture

Four stages of HR Tech Market

Systems of Record	Systems of Talent	Systems of Engagement	Systems of Work
• 1970s – 1980s • Focus on transaction and record-keeping • Mainframe and client/server • Ran on PCs • Data warehouse • HR, Payroll, and Finance	• 1990s – 2000s • Focus on recruiting, performance, talent management • Automation • Mobile and Social • Analytics • Used by HOD, Recruiting, Learning, and Line Managers	• 2000s – till today • Cloud-based HCM platforms • UX/UI • Mobile and Social first • Analytics embedded into the application • Used by HR, Managers and Employees	• 2021 – till date • Employee journeys, interactions, and everyday needs • Integrated with Teams, Workplace, Salesforce, Slack • Cloud-based, Mobile-design, consumer-grade • AI-embedded • Used by HR, Managers, Employees, and contractors

Table 4: Evolution of the HR Tech Market

AI is now here

1. Core HR: Recommended salary adjustments, job changes, career moves, span of control, compliance trends
2. Recruitment: Intelligent sourcing, candidate marketing, video and audio interviewing, chatbots for candidate screening, assessment, and tracking interview processes
3. Learning: Inferred skills, recommended content, recommended programs, recommended adjacent skills, recommended types of content. AI-based coach matching, AI-based virtual reality training, AI-based microlearning, AI-based peer assessment
4. Diversity and Inclusion: Identifying and reducing bias in job descriptions, candidate communications, interview patterns, pay, rewards, promotion, and mobility
5. Management and Leadership: AI-based nudges, action plans, learning recommendations, and tips based on engagement surveys, assessments, and feedback from teammates
6. Career and Mobility: Recommended gigs, new roles, new developmental assignments
7. Organizational Design: ONA (organizational network analysis) to identify strong influencers, patterns of strong or weak teamwork, micromanagement, non-diverse or non-inclusive communications
8. Wellbeing and Productivity: Time spent in meetings, time wasted in unproductive meetings, tracking of motion, health metrics, exercise, sleep, diagnosis of mental health, AI-assignment of psychologists or medical practitioners
9. HR Service Delivery: AI-based chatbots with ever-increasing intelligence to answer questions, assist with employee journeys, remove need for HR administrators and robotic process automation to automate most routine transaction processing

Experience economy

Let us look at some of the leading practices and trends that drive HR related activities in the experience economy.

Candidate experience

Candidates expect their application experiences to mirror the online shopping experience.

Onboarding experience

Virtually meet team/coworkers. Access social network of employees – connections & relevant content

Team engagement

Align culture & management practices with workforce eco-system including external talent

Tools and Access

Employees want their business applications to be like consumer applications

Learning & Development

Competency-based development goals to upskill the workforce. Internal and external content for self-based learning.

Performance

O + X = Connecting Operational Data (O) with Experience Data (X). Continuous feedback through improved listening programs

Leaves

Invest in the well-being of the employee. A competitive advantage in today's economy is a positive engaged workforce.

Rewards & Recognition

Benefits package based on what's important to your employees.

Travel

Employees have real-time access to information from anywhere.

Roles & KRA

Derive insights using Machine Learning and Natural Language Processing, to help next-generation leaders achieve their full potential

Exit

Exit feedback & other employee touchpoints to steer employee lifecycle improvements

Rethinking ground-up

As CIO or the CHRO, there is a need to rethink about the common issues faced by the HR function. Devise digital employee themes and strategies for digital employees.

Common HR pain-points

1. Understand employee touchpoints that matter
2. Ways to drive engagement
3. Listen & capture Voice of Employee
4. Customer & Employee Experience are intertwined
5. Making sense of massive data
6. Analytics and Insights
7. Selecting a Technology Platform
8. Want to see changes based on feedback

Digital employee themes and strategies

1. Employee expectations: Understand every experience that matters to your employees
    a. Company culture focuses on transparency, meaningful work, individual development, inclusion, innovation, autonomy, collaboration
    b. Employee experience must be measurable & leadership driven
    c. Intuitive, automated, analytical platform

2. Digital Open Door: End-to-end listening technology designed to create conversations in moments that matter
    a. Employees, anonymous, feedback and submit issues
    b. Ad-hoc surveys on internal programs
    c. Quantitative measures for predictive modelling
    d. Event-based feedback across the employee lifecycle

3. X+O Insights: Real-time insight into what is happening (O-data) to impact engagement as well as the why (X-data)
    a. Connect employee experience across other core experiences – customer experience, brand experience, and product experience

4. Intelligent Action Plans: Automatic recommendations & action plans that link to key drivers and areas identified in need of improvement
    a. Intelligent features – key driver analysis, native text analysis, ML, and predictive AI
    b. Real-time insight into which behaviors are trending across your organization. Drive development. Create a motivated & productive workforce.

Digital HR Core

There is a need for organizations to have digital technology at the core of HR function, where everything in the organization comes together to transform how you manage your workforce for business goals and success.

1. Workforce Data: A single view across geographies, cost centers, and employee types
2. Intuitive Tools: Form groups, and network. Share knowledge across interests, work experience, and locations. Intuitive Time & Attendance
3. Intelligent services: Personalized & consistent service delivery for employees, managers, and HR
4. Reporting Tools: Support Trending & drill-down analyses. Embedded analytics
5. Integration Capabilities: Integration with on-premise and cloud solutions (e.g. integration with external labor and services procurement)

Flexible & Global HR Core

The new HR mandate propagates going beyond automating processes, reducing costs, and ensuring compliance to building purposeful relationships across the business to create a modern and engaging workplace. Connected HR processes enabling you to attract, develop, and retain employees using Digital. This will enhance everyday work life, providing employees with a consumer-grade employee experience powered by live insights to help them make data-driven decisions. Standardized HR processes focused on the entire workforce (including external labor). Increase workforce productivity with self-service that provides fast, intuitive access to important tasks across all devices. Real-time insight into your entire workforce.

Digital recruiting, hiring, and onboarding

1. Optimal workforce to meet business objectives: Workforce plans to meet increasing competitive pressures, digitalization, and rapidly evolving business and organizational strategies

    a. Develop strategies that help ensure you hire and retain the right talent for years to come
    b. Strategic Workforce Planning
    c. Operation Headcount Planning
    d. Plan for changing organizational needs and transform into an ongoing planning practice
    e. "What-If" Modelling: To impact employee hiring, development, and retention decisions
    f. Analytics: By job, source, and campaign, to optimize spend.

2. Getting the right talent: Source, engage, and hire the world's best talent.

    a. Search engine-optimized career site to increase candidate flow
    b. Source Talent
    c. Engage with active, passive, internal & external candidates
    d. Nurture candidate relationships
    e. Mobile experience eliminates wait times to fill positions faster
    f. Simplify Hiring
    g. Mobile: Keep things flowing for candidates, recruiters, managers & employees on the go

3. Onboarding: Create a personalized onboarding experience for new hires

    a. People: Virtually meet their team and a handpicked group of coworkers and introduce themselves.
    b. Process: Step-by-step wizards to walk hiring managers through the process of how to prepare for the new hire.

c. Productivity: Productivity is key even as new hires, managers and HR are busy and have different goals in onboarding
d. Social network: New hires have access to social network of employees, build connections & consume relevant content
e. LMS: Creating an aligned & trained new hire.

Digital Social Collaboration

1. First day at job: Social collaboration will connect employees to the experts & information. Provide content and people recommendations based on their employee profile. Onboarding groups enable employees to easily share information and experiences.
2. Continuous learning: Tap into employees' natural learning styles. Use discovery, collaboration, peer resources, and expert findings. Helping employees find new and inventive ways to get answers and further their on-the-job learning experience.
3. Building relationships: Increase employee engagement by enabling mentoring relationships, and connecting employees and peer-recognized experts. Share knowledge in one-to-one or one-to-many relationships.
4. Collaboration templates: Pre-built work patterns for education, training, information sharing, mentoring, coaching, and bringing together people, data, and processes. These templates expedite the creation and streamline ongoing collaboration
5. Cross-company communication: Announce goals and initiatives and keep everyone up to date with the latest materials. Create an internal community to guide employees through new processes and allow members to ask questions and get expert responses.
6. Collaboration: Share, view, download, and annotate files, images, and videos. Public and private groups to bring the right audience for what needs to be accomplished. External collaboration brings customers, partners, vendors, and suppliers into your internal collaboration

Mobilize HR

1. Employee Information:
   - *Employees can access and edit profiles to ensure that all information is current and correct.*
   - *Ensure that the HR department has the latest information about employee skills and qualifications*
   - *Stay updated about your earnings*

2. Self-service:
   - *Managers can complete administrative HR tasks on the move*
   - *Review talent profiles, including skills, performance history, competencies, and development objectives*
   - *Connect with your direct reports by e-mails, calls, or text messages*

3. Approval on the go:
   - *To-do-list for managers to review requests for approvals*
   - *Submit job requisitions, providing interview feedback, completing performance reviews, submitting approvals for time off or training, and submitting job transfer authorizations.*

4. Organizational relationships:
   - *View organizational structure on your screen. Touch capability to access employee profiles.*
   - *Search functionality that remembers frequent searches and sync suggestion lists across multiple devices.*

5. Business decisions:
   - *Managers access relevant and timely workforce analytics and insights.*
   - *Instant view into workforce issues and concerns for your organization while drilling down to identify likely root causes and related risk areas.*

Move to cloud

1. Low TCO: No big up-front costs, no upgrade or 3rd party license costs, and no maintenance costs.
2. Automatic updates: Customers don't need to bother with installations or updates.
3. Assurance: No concerns about speed, downtime, and disaster recovery.
4. Rapid deployment: You can be up and running quickly
5. User experience: Easy, browser-based access, an intuitive interface you can customize easily
6. Security and compliance: No concerns over the security of physical premises as well as technical security on the access, application, and network levels. Compliance is always up-to-date
7. Extensibility: Out-of-the-box features and functionality are great, but you need to be able to further configure and customize your apps to your needs

CHAPTER 10

HR ANALYTICS

Question

How can we analyze all the data that digital HR will create within the organization? What are the measures and metrics that we can use as HR professionals to analyze and report? An exhaustive list of measures and metrics is provided in this chapter, with the formulas to calculate them.

Strategic management

- HR Expense to revenue ratio = Total HR expenses ÷ Revenue
- HR Expenses to FTE= HR expenses ÷ Total No. of FTEs
- HR to workers ratio = (HR FTEs ÷ Total Number of FTEs in the organization)×100
- Break-even Point The point in time when costs invested in developing or improving an HR program is equal to or greater than the returns. In other words, the break-even point is reached when returns to-date are equal to investments.

    - Formula: Development cost/Annual return
    - Example: A new on-line training program has a development cost of $100,000. It is expected to generate a return of $50,000 in reduced delivery costs each year.
    - Break-even point = $100,000 /$50,000 = 2 years

- Cost-Benefit Ratio: How the Benefits of a program or activity relate to the Costs associated with developing and executing that program or activity. When you are calculating Costs for any HR program be clear as to what you have included. In our example here we have included the salary + benefit costs for a new program lead and the use of a consultant to help develop the new program and make the systems changes to our HRIS necessary to capture Successor and High Potential identification. We have not included the cost of the time of managers and HRBPs to participate in the program.

- o Example: The new succession management program will produce a savings of $500,000 in reduced search firm fees over the targeted time frame (2 years) and will cost $250,000 to develop and manage over that same period.
- o Cost-benefit ratio = $500,000:$250,000 = 2:1
- o Total Cost-Benefit ratio is 2 to 1.

- ROI (Return on Investment): The return on a company's monetary investment in a new program or activity or change to a current program or activity. The measurement of ROI can be calculated in several ways. If your organization has a standard formula, it's best to use that formula. If not, this formula can work for most situations. Anticipated Benefits can be ascertained by looking at potential reductions in the costs of administering and delivering the program (e.g., reduced vendor fees, lower headcount needed to administer), increases in productivity, or reductions in costs enabled by the methodology or other aspects of the program (e.g., less time away from work and reduced travel expenses by putting a program online), and improved outcomes (e.g., reducing turnover and employee relations issues, and increasing employee productivity with a better leadership program). Quantify these benefits as much as possible. Costs and Benefits must be calculated for a set period of time that represents a reasonable lifetime for the program. A complete ROI analysis should also highlight those benefits that cannot be financially quantified but still represent desired outcomes.

- o   Formula ((Anticipated Benefits – Total Development Cost of Program)/ Total Development Cost of Program) x 100

Workforce Planning and Staffing

- Contingent Representation Rate = (Contingent headcount FTEs ÷ Total Workforce FTEs) x 100
- Cost of Turnover and Cost per Turnover = (Total of the costs of separation + vacancy + replacement Turnover costs) ÷ No. of positions filled due to separation
- Cost Per Hire = Total costs related to all external hires ÷ Number of external hires
- Turnover ratio = No. of employees left ÷ (Beginning + Ending No. of Employees/2) × 100
- Offer declines ratio = (No. of declines ÷ No. of offers extended) × 100
- Percentage of exceptions processed for payroll, benefits, promotions, and other HR This metric is helpful to understand the amount of special effort required to process benefits, promotions, and other HR transactions that are out of the standard protocol.

  - o   Formula: Total number of exceptions processed by HR ÷ all HR transactions

- Turnover Rate: Rate at which employees are leaving the organization in a given time period. It is suggested that Turnover be categorized as Employer Intended vs Employer Unintended, and the latter category be further divided into Voluntary and All Others. The objective of measuring turnover is to determine where and when the organization has risk of losing talent that it doesn't want to lose, and to determine how to mitigate that risk. Therefore identifying Employer Intended separations segments out of that risk analysis terminations for poor performance or cause, layoffs or job eliminations, acceptance of early retirement offers, etc. which are irrelevant to identifying and mitigating the risk. Identifying Voluntary (resignation and retirement) separately from other Employer Unintended, like death, incarceration, job abandonment, refusal to accept new assignment, etc. also helps to focus our risk analysis. The Voluntary category is the most relevant to the Turnover risk analysis. Turnover of New Hires and Failure to Start Rate are also good metrics for Staffing professionals to be measuring. Other Turnover subgroups are important to other areas of analysis and decision making. For example, Turnover of Poor Performers can provide insight into the effectiveness of your Performance Management. Turnover rates are also useful inputs into Workforce Planning. The reporting of overall turnover is no longer considered best practice. This metric is unlikely to inform and improve decision making. Focus on key employee populations: Top Performers, New Hires, Poor Performers, Successors, High Potentials, Key Positions, High Risk Employees. These are the groups worth acting on if Turnover becomes unacceptable.

- o Formula: (Number of separations during the time period ÷ average actual number of employees during the time period) x 100.
- o Time periods – typically year, quarter, month, pay period

- Cost Per Hire: Average cost incurred with an external hire. Total costs should include the sum of all direct costs (e.g., advertising, hiring events, agencies, search firms, employee referral programs, onboarding and travel for applicants and interviewers) incurred in attracting and hiring employees. Some organizations also include relocation costs, interviewer pay, and staffing department operating expenses. If the HR interviewers have other responsibilities like internal hiring or generalist duties then pay would need to be pro-rated for the time involved in external recruiting. If you include management interviewers you would also need to pro-rate pay since they have many other duties.

- Formula: Total costs related to all external hires/ Number of external hires
- Retention: Degree to which an organization is retaining key employees. As an example, this can tell you what the retention rate of University Relations hires is at 1, 3, and 5 years of service and whether the rate is different for different Universities or for those that interned with your organization vs those that did not.

  o Formula: # of employees in the selected group employed at the designated time/ # of employees in that selected group originally

- Offer Rate: Percentage of applicants interviewed that receive offers.
- Formula: (Total number of candidates offered ÷ number of candidates interviewed) x 100

Talent Management

- Training Participation Rate = (Number of employees who participated in at least one company paid training activity ÷ Number of employees eligible for training) x 100
- Training Spend Rates = (Training spend ÷ Total Human Capital Spend) x 100
- Average Training Hours = Total training hours ÷ total number of workers participating in training
- Performance Review Completion Rate = (Number of completed performance reviews ÷ Number of completed performance reviews due) x 100

Total Rewards

- Total Compensation Spend Rate= ((Direct compensation + Indirect compensation) ÷ Total operating spend) x 100
- Health Care Spend Rate = Total health care expenses ÷ number of employees enrolled in a health care plan
- Benefit Participation Rate= (Number of employees participating in Plan or Program ÷ Number of employees eligible for Plan or Program) x 100

Risk Management

- Accidents =Number of accidents.
- Accidents to employee ratio=Number of accidents/ Number of employees

Financial Management

- Revenue per Total Human Capital (HC) $pend The total amount of revenue received during an organization's fiscal year divided by the total spend on Human Capital. This ratio conceptually links the costs associated with the firm's human capital to its productivity. If the revenue-per-THCS ratio increases, it indicates that there is greater efficiency and productivity because more output is being produced per $ spent on human capital. If the ratio decreases, it indicates there is less efficiency and productivity. Total Human Capital Spend should include wages, benefits; independent contractors, temps and other non-employee workers; and, HR program costs (non-staff) including outsourcing.

  - Formula: Revenue ÷ Total HC $pend

- Revenue Per FTE: The Total Revenue divided by the number of FTEs. This ratio conceptually measures the efficiency and productive use of human capital because it links the time and effort associated with the firm's human capital to its revenue output. If the revenue-per-FTE ratio increases, it might indicate that more output is being produced per FTE. However, if it increases due primarily to major declines in FTEs from involuntary staff reductions or increased outsourcing, this may be misleading. The metric can temporarily look like increased efficiency or productivity. If revenue is not sustained over time with the lower staff levels then productivity and/or efficiency have not actually improved.

- o   Formula Revenue ÷ number of FTEs

- Productivity: Describes the relationship between real output and the amount of labor time involved in its production.

  - o   Formula: Revenue/ Labor hour

Succession planning

- Succession Fill Rate: Degree to which your Succession Management program is providing viable candidates for successor positions.

  - o   Formula: (Number of succession positions filled with a Successor/ Number of succession positions filled) x 100

- Successor and High Potential Retention Degree to which you are retaining those employees who are successors, and those who have been assessed as having the potential to be successors.

  - o   Formula: (Number of Successor or High Potential employees at the targeted time period/Number of Successor or High Potential employees originally) x 100

Employee Engagement

- Employee Engagement: Degree to which employees are engaged with and committed to the strategy and objectives of the organization, and demonstrate their commitment to organization's success through the contribution of their skills, knowledge, abilities, and performance.

  - Formula: There is no one way to measure Engagement. Many companies use surveys. However, surveys have challenges – self-reporting can be flawed, participation is typically not 100% and is skewed to favor engaged vs non-engaged employees, output is dated since surveys are often done only annually, and they reflect attitudes or opinions not necessarily behavior. Each organization must drive a metric that reflects employee behavioral alignment with its unique strategy and objectives.

CHAPTER 11

EMPLOYEE ENGAGEMENT

Question

Employee engagement is a crucial strategy for organizations seeking to secure a competitive edge in today's fast-paced and ever-evolving business environment. Unlike tangible assets or proprietary technologies, the human element within a company—its employees—represents a unique and invaluable resource. While competitors can replicate products, technologies, or even business models, they cannot easily replicate a company's distinct culture, values, or the specific contributions of its engaged workforce.

Employee engagement encompasses the level of commitment, enthusiasm, and emotional investment that employees have toward their organization and its goals. Engaged employees are not just satisfied with their jobs; they are deeply involved in their work, motivated to go beyond the call of duty, and invested in the success of the organization. This high level of engagement can lead to a multitude of positive outcomes for a company, including increased productivity, enhanced customer satisfaction, and improved overall performance.

One of the most significant advantages of fostering employee engagement is its impact on organizational performance. Engaged employees are more likely to put forth discretionary effort, which means they are willing to do more than what is strictly required of them. This can manifest in various ways, such as coming up with innovative solutions to problems, delivering superior customer service, or contributing to a positive workplace culture. Such behaviors not only improve the efficiency and effectiveness of the organization but also help in building a strong and differentiated brand reputation.

Moreover, engaged employees tend to have higher levels of job satisfaction and are less likely to leave the company. High employee turnover can be costly for organizations, leading to increased recruitment and training expenses, as well as potential disruptions in productivity. By contrast, when employees are engaged, they are more likely to remain with the company and contribute to its long-term success. This stability is essential for maintaining continuity and fostering a knowledgeable and skilled workforce.

Another critical aspect of employee engagement is its role in fostering innovation and adaptability. In a rapidly changing business landscape, organizations must continuously evolve to stay ahead of their competitors. Engaged employees are more likely to embrace change, contribute innovative ideas, and drive the organization forward. Their intrinsic motivation and commitment to the company's goals make them more agile and responsive to new challenges and opportunities.

Furthermore, employee engagement can significantly impact customer satisfaction and loyalty. Employees who are engaged are more likely to provide exceptional service and create positive interactions with customers. This can lead to enhanced customer experiences, higher levels of customer retention, and ultimately, a stronger competitive position in the market.

Investing in employee engagement involves implementing strategies that promote a positive work environment, recognize and reward contributions, and provide opportunities for personal and professional growth. It requires a commitment from leadership to create a culture where employees feel valued, heard, and empowered. This investment not only enhances the well-being and satisfaction of employees but also drives organizational success.

In summary, employee engagement is an invaluable tool for organizations seeking to gain a competitive advantage. By effectively managing and engaging their workforce, companies can harness the unique strengths and contributions of their employees, leading to improved performance, higher employee retention, increased innovation, and enhanced customer satisfaction. In a world where competitors can imitate products and services, the genuine commitment and enthusiasm of a dedicated workforce remain a distinctive and powerful asset that can set an organization apart.

Determinants of employee engagement

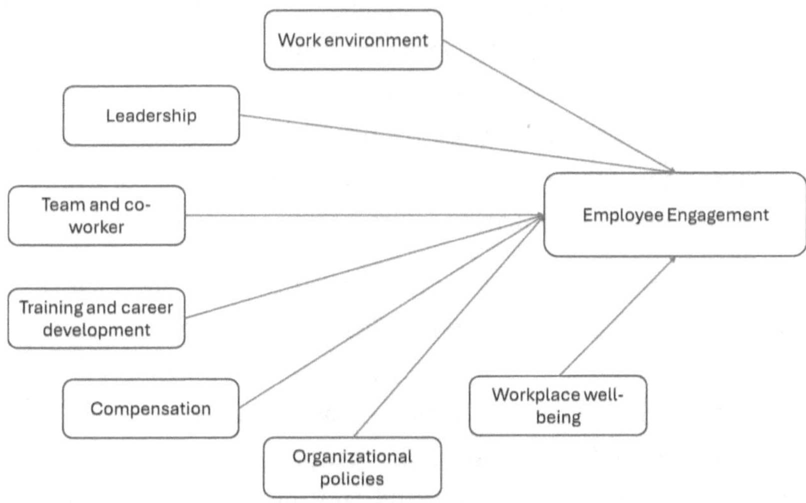

Figure 11: Determinants of employee engagement

Work environment

A positive work environment plays a crucial role in fostering employee engagement and overall job satisfaction. When management creates a supportive atmosphere, it demonstrates a genuine concern for employees' needs and well-being. This approach involves actively listening to employees, offering constructive feedback, and encouraging open communication. Such an environment not only addresses employees' immediate concerns but also promotes their personal and professional development.

A supportive work environment is characterized by several key elements that contribute to employee engagement. Firstly, management's concern for employees' needs and feelings is paramount. This involves understanding and addressing issues such as work-life balance, job security, and personal challenges that may affect employees' performance and satisfaction. When employees feel that their managers genuinely care about their well-being, they are more likely to feel valued and motivated.

Secondly, providing positive feedback is essential in fostering a supportive environment. Recognizing and celebrating employees' achievements and contributions helps to boost their morale and motivation. Positive reinforcement not only encourages employees to maintain high performance but also builds their confidence and commitment to the organization.

Encouraging employees to voice their concerns is another crucial aspect of a supportive work environment. When employees feel comfortable sharing their thoughts and opinions, it creates a sense of trust and transparency within the organization. This openness can lead to better problem-solving and innovation, as employees are more likely to contribute their ideas and solutions when they feel heard and respected.

Moreover, a supportive work environment promotes opportunities for employees to develop new skills and advance their careers. Offering training programs, mentorship, and career development opportunities helps employees grow professionally and personally. This investment in their development not only enhances their skill set but also increases their engagement and loyalty to the organization.

Solving work-related problems collaboratively is another important feature of a supportive work environment. When employees are encouraged to work together to address challenges, it fosters teamwork and enhances interpersonal relationships. This collaborative approach not only improves problem-solving efficiency but also strengthens the sense of camaraderie and trust among team members.

A meaningful workplace environment that supports focused work and interpersonal harmony is a key determinant of employee engagement. Such an environment allows employees to concentrate on their tasks without unnecessary stress or distractions, leading to increased productivity and job satisfaction. Additionally, harmonious interpersonal relationships contribute to a positive workplace culture, where employees feel comfortable and valued.

In summary, a supportive work environment is vital for enhancing employee engagement. Management's concern for employees' needs, the provision of positive feedback, encouragement to voice concerns, opportunities for skill development, and collaborative problem-solving all contribute to a meaningful and engaging workplace. By creating such an environment, organizations can foster greater employee commitment, satisfaction, and overall performance, ultimately leading to a more successful and competitive business.

Leadership

Leadership is a fundamental driver of employee engagement, with effective leaders naturally inspiring and motivating their teams. The role of leaders extends beyond merely managing day-to-day operations; they are pivotal in shaping the organizational culture and fostering an environment where employees feel valued and driven.

A key aspect of leadership that impacts engagement is the ability to communicate the significance of employees' contributions to the overall success of the business. When leaders clearly articulate how individual and team efforts align with and support the organization's goals, employees are more likely to see the value and purpose in their work. This sense of purpose not only motivates employees but also deepens their commitment to their roles and the organization as a whole.

Inspiring leaders create an environment where employees understand that their work is important and meaningful. This recognition and appreciation contribute significantly to employee engagement. When employees perceive their tasks as integral to the company's success and are acknowledged for their contributions, they are more likely to invest their energy and enthusiasm into their roles. This engagement is further fuelled by the leaders' ability to convey a compelling vision and set clear, achievable goals that resonate with employees.

Authentic and supportive leadership plays a crucial role in enhancing employee engagement. Authentic leaders are genuine, transparent, and consistent in their interactions with employees. They build trust and credibility by demonstrating integrity, honesty, and a genuine interest in their team's well-being. This authenticity fosters a strong connection between leaders and employees, creating a supportive environment where employees feel safe to express their ideas and concerns.

Supportive leadership involves actively listening to employees, providing constructive feedback, and offering encouragement and recognition. Leaders who are approachable and responsive to their team's needs help create a positive work environment where employees feel valued and motivated. This support not only enhances job satisfaction but also promotes a collaborative and inclusive culture, where employees are more engaged and committed to their work.

The impact of leadership on employee engagement is evident in increased involvement, satisfaction, and enthusiasm for work. Leaders who are able to inspire and support their teams effectively can significantly enhance employee engagement levels. Engaged employees are more likely to demonstrate higher levels of productivity, creativity, and dedication, contributing to the organization's overall success.

In summary, effective leadership is central to fostering employee engagement. Leaders who communicate the importance of employees' contributions, provide a sense of purpose, and exhibit authenticity and support can significantly enhance employee involvement and satisfaction. By creating an inspiring and supportive work environment, leaders can drive higher levels of engagement, leading to a more motivated and committed workforce, and ultimately, to the organization's greater success.

Team and co-worker relationship

Creating an open and supportive environment is crucial for fostering a workplace where employees feel secure and fully engaged in their responsibilities. Such an environment not only enhances job satisfaction but also drives greater levels of creativity, innovation, and productivity.

An open and supportive workplace is characterized by its approach to communication, feedback, and risk-taking. When employees feel that their workplace is open and accepting, they are more likely to express their ideas, voice their concerns, and participate actively in organizational activities. This openness facilitates transparent dialogue between employees and management, ensuring that concerns are addressed promptly and that employees feel heard and valued.

Supportive environments are particularly important in allowing employees to experiment and try new approaches without the fear of negative repercussions. Innovation often involves taking risks and exploring uncharted territory, and a supportive workplace encourages this by creating a culture where experimentation is viewed as a valuable part of growth rather than something to be punished. Employees who are confident that they will not face severe consequences for unsuccessful attempts are more likely to engage in creative problem-solving and propose novel ideas that can drive the organization forward.

The ability to try new things and even fail is a crucial element in a supportive work environment. Failure, when managed constructively, can be an important learning opportunity. In a supportive culture, failures are not seen as personal shortcomings but as steps in the learning process. This perspective helps employees to approach challenges with a growth mindset, where the focus is on learning from mistakes and improving future performance. Such an environment fosters resilience and adaptability, qualities that are essential for both personal and organizational success.

Moreover, a supportive environment also involves recognizing and celebrating successes, no matter how small. Positive reinforcement and acknowledgment of achievements contribute to a sense of accomplishment and motivation. Employees who feel appreciated are more likely to remain engaged and committed to their work. This recognition also reinforces the value of experimentation and risk-taking, encouraging employees to continue pushing boundaries and striving for excellence.

In summary, an open and supportive work environment is fundamental for employees to feel safe, engaged, and motivated. By promoting transparency, encouraging experimentation, and handling failures constructively, organizations can create a culture that not only supports but also actively enhances employee engagement and innovation. This environment empowers employees to fully embrace their responsibilities, contributing to overall organizational success and fostering a dynamic and forward-thinking workplace.

Training and career development

When employees participate in training and development programs, it significantly enhances their confidence and engagement in their roles. These programs are crucial not only for acquiring new skills but also for reinforcing the employee's sense of capability and motivation. When employees feel that they are growing and advancing, their connection to their job and organization strengthens, leading to higher levels of engagement.

Training and development initiatives play a pivotal role in building employee confidence. As employees gain new skills and knowledge, they become more proficient in their tasks and responsibilities. This increased competence naturally boosts their self-esteem and encourages them to tackle their roles with greater enthusiasm. Confidence is a key driver of engagement because when employees are assured of their abilities, they are more likely to take initiative, contribute innovative ideas, and commit fully to their work.

Furthermore, it is essential for management to prioritize the career development paths of their employees. A well-structured career path, supported by continuous training and development, provides employees with clear goals and aspirations. When employees see that their career progression is supported and that there are opportunities for advancement, they are more likely to remain motivated and engaged. This structured approach helps employees envision their future within the organization, fostering a sense of loyalty and long-term commitment.

Providing timely opportunities for growth and development is another critical factor in enhancing employee engagement. When employees are given access to relevant training and development programs, they are better equipped to meet the evolving demands of their roles. This proactive approach not only prepares employees for future challenges but also ensures that they are continually developing skills that are valuable to both their personal career goals and the organization's objectives.

Moreover, when employees perceive that their organization is invested in their growth, they are more likely to reciprocate with increased engagement and dedication. Training and development opportunities signal to employees that their contributions are valued and that the organization is committed to their success. This recognition and support contribute to a positive work environment where employees feel appreciated and motivated to perform at their best.

In summary, training and development programs are instrumental in boosting employee confidence and engagement. By offering structured career development paths and timely growth opportunities, management can enhance employees' skills, increase their confidence, and foster a deeper commitment to their roles. This investment in employee development not only improves individual performance but also contributes to overall organizational success by creating a more engaged and capable workforce.

Compensation

Compensation and remuneration are fundamental elements that significantly influence employee engagement. An effective compensation strategy not only motivates employees to excel but also fosters their dedication to both work and personal development. This encompasses a blend of financial and non-financial rewards that collectively contribute to an employee's overall job satisfaction and engagement.

Financial rewards, including salary, bonuses, and other monetary incentives, are crucial for motivating employees. Competitive pay ensures that employees feel their contributions are valued and fairly rewarded. Bonuses and performance-based incentives further encourage employees to strive for excellence by linking their efforts directly to tangible benefits. These financial rewards are essential for attracting and retaining talent, as they provide a direct correlation between performance and compensation.

However, non-financial rewards also play a significant role in shaping employee engagement. Benefits such as extra holiday time, flexible working arrangements, and various employee discount schemes can enhance job satisfaction and work-life balance. Non-financial rewards often address employees' personal needs and preferences, which can be as impactful as financial incentives in boosting morale and motivation.

The effectiveness of a compensation strategy is heavily influenced by employees' perceptions of their rewards. It is not merely the quantity or type of reward that matters, but how employees perceive these rewards in relation to their expectations and needs. For instance, an employee might value additional time off more than a small bonus, or they might prioritize professional development opportunities over monetary incentives. Therefore, management must understand and address the diverse preferences of their workforce to tailor compensation packages that resonate with employees.

Moreover, the presentation and implementation of compensation and recognition programs are critical. Clear communication about how rewards are determined and how they align with performance can help manage expectations and enhance employee satisfaction. Transparency in these processes ensures that employees feel fairly treated and understand the link between their efforts and the rewards they receive.

Management should strive to establish acceptable standards of remuneration and recognition to achieve high levels of employee engagement. This means regularly reviewing and updating compensation packages to stay competitive within the industry and align with the evolving needs of employees. Engaging with employees to gather feedback on their compensation and recognition preferences can also provide valuable insights into how to refine these programs effectively.

In summary, compensation and remuneration are vital components of employee engagement. An effective compensation strategy involves a mix of financial rewards, such as salary and bonuses, along with non-financial rewards, like additional leave and flexible working options. Ultimately, it is the employees' perceptions of these rewards that determine their engagement levels. Management must, therefore, present fair and appealing standards of remuneration and recognition to foster a highly engaged and motivated workforce.

Organizational policies

Organizational policies, procedures, structures, and systems play a crucial role in determining the level of employee engagement within a company. These elements not only shape the day-to-day working environment but also influence how employees perceive their roles and their commitment to the organization. Research consistently shows that well-designed organizational policies and procedures are essential for fostering a high level of employee engagement and achieving business goals.

Fair Recruitment and Selection

- One of the foundational policies that impact employee engagement is a fair recruitment and selection process. Transparent and equitable hiring practices ensure that all candidates are given an equal opportunity based on their skills and qualifications. When employees feel that the recruitment process is just and that promotions are based on merit, it fosters a sense of fairness and trust within the organization. This trust is crucial for maintaining high levels of engagement, as employees who believe in the integrity of their organization are more likely to be motivated and committed.

Flexible Working Arrangements

- Another significant factor is the implementation of flexible working arrangements. Policies that support flexi-timing, remote work, and other forms of work-life balance are highly valued by employees. Such arrangements allow employees to manage their professional responsibilities alongside personal commitments more effectively. Organizations that offer flexibility are often seen as more accommodating and supportive, which can greatly enhance employee satisfaction and engagement. Flexibility in work arrangements helps employees to balance their work and personal lives, reducing stress and increasing their overall well-being.

Support for Work-Life Balance

- Policies that aid in balancing work and life are increasingly important in today's fast-paced world. Organizations that provide support for employees to manage their work and personal lives, such as parental leave, mental health days, and wellness programs, demonstrate a commitment to employee well-being. This support not only helps employees to remain engaged by alleviating stress and burnout but also fosters a positive work environment where employees feel valued and cared for.

Fair Promotional Policies

- Fair and transparent promotional policies also play a critical role in employee engagement. Employees are more likely to be engaged when they perceive that career advancement is based on clear criteria and performance rather than favoritism or arbitrary decisions. Implementing fair promotional practices ensures that employees see a clear pathway for their career growth and are motivated to contribute their best efforts to achieve both their personal career goals and the organization's objectives.

Organizational Structures and Systems

- The overall organizational structure and systems also impact employee engagement. Efficient, well-defined systems for communication, feedback, and support help employees to understand their roles and how they fit into the larger organizational framework. Clear organizational structures facilitate better coordination and collaboration, which can enhance job satisfaction and engagement.

- Organizational policies, procedures, structures, and systems significantly influence employee engagement. Fair recruitment and selection, flexible working arrangements, support for work-life balance, and equitable promotional policies are critical components that contribute to a supportive work environment. By adopting and maintaining policies that address these areas effectively, organizations can create an environment where employees are motivated, satisfied, and engaged, ultimately driving the achievement of business goals.

Workplace well-being

- Wellbeing encompasses all aspects of how individuals perceive and experience their lives, including their physical health, mental state, emotional satisfaction, and overall quality of life. In the context of the workplace, wellbeing is crucial for employee engagement because it affects how employees feel about their jobs and their overall life satisfaction.

- A key driver of employee engagement is the genuine interest and commitment of senior management towards employee wellbeing. When senior leaders prioritize and actively support the wellbeing of their employees, it has a profound impact on engagement levels across the organization.

The Role of Senior Management in Employee Wellbeing

Senior management's interest in employee wellbeing is a critical factor that shapes organizational culture and employee engagement. When leadership demonstrates a genuine commitment to the health and happiness of their employees, it sets a positive tone throughout the organization. This commitment can be manifested in several ways:

1. Policy and Program Development: Senior management can champion the development and implementation of policies and programs designed to enhance employee wellbeing. This might include health and wellness initiatives, mental health support, work-life balance programs, and stress management resources. By prioritizing these areas, management not only addresses employees' immediate needs but also demonstrates a long-term commitment to their overall quality of life.

2. Resource Allocation: Effective wellbeing initiatives require adequate resources, including budgetary support and dedicated personnel. Senior management's allocation of resources towards wellbeing programs indicates that employee health and satisfaction are valued priorities. This investment helps ensure that wellbeing programs are well-executed and can have a meaningful impact on employees' lives.

3. Communication and Support: Transparent communication about the importance of wellbeing and the resources available to employees is essential. Senior leaders who openly discuss wellbeing initiatives and actively support employees in utilizing these resources help to foster a culture of care and support. This approach encourages employees to engage with wellbeing programs and seek assistance when needed.

4. Role Modeling and Culture: Leadership plays a crucial role in modeling behaviors that reflect the organization's commitment to wellbeing. When senior leaders prioritize their own health and demonstrate work-life balance, they set an example for employees. This role modeling helps to normalize wellbeing practices and encourages employees to adopt similar habits.

5. Feedback and Continuous Improvement: Engaged senior management is also attentive to feedback from employees regarding wellbeing programs and policies. By actively seeking and responding to employee feedback, leadership can continuously improve and adapt wellbeing initiatives to better

meet the needs of the workforce. This responsiveness shows employees that their wellbeing is a top priority and helps to build trust and engagement.

Impact on Employee Engagement

When senior management shows a genuine interest in employee wellbeing, it creates a supportive and positive work environment. Employees who feel that their leaders care about their wellbeing are more likely to be engaged, motivated, and committed to their roles. They are also more likely to experience higher levels of job satisfaction and overall life satisfaction, which translates into better performance and lower turnover rates.

Senior management's commitment to employee wellbeing is a crucial driver of engagement. By prioritizing wellbeing through policies, resources, communication, role modeling, and feedback, senior leaders can foster a positive work environment that enhances employee satisfaction and engagement. This commitment not only improves the overall quality of life for employees but also contributes to the organization's success by creating a motivated and dedicated workforce.

REFERENCES

- The Human Resource Architecture: Toward a Theory of Human Capital Allocation and Development Author(s): David P. Lepak and Scott A. Snell
- SHRM
- Organizational Climate and Culture Benjamin Schneider, Mark G. Ehrhart, and William H. Macey
- HR factors for the successful implementation of Industry 4.0: A systematic literature review. Anju Verma and Murugesan Venkatesan
- Maximizing Your Return on People – HBR
- Human Resources (HR) Toolkit for Small and Medium Nonprofit Actors – Cornerstone
- A guide to conducting behavioral interviews with early career job candidates – SHRM
- Human Resource Planning – Newfoundland Labrador
- IIM Shillong
- HR Metrics – SHRM
- Determinants of employee engagement and their impact on employee performance. Anitha J. IJPPM.
- Human Resource Management by Gary Dessler
- Armstrong's Handbook of Human Resource Management Practice by Michael Armstrong
- The New HR Leader's First 100 Days by Alan Collins
- Human Resources Professional Association (HRPA): www.hrpa.ca
- CIPD (Chartered Institute of Personnel and Development): www.cipd.co.uk

- Journal of Human Resource Management
- Academy of Management Journal
- International Journal of Human Resource Management
- Harvard Business Review (HBR): www.hbr.org
- Forbes HR Section: www.forbes.com/hr
- LinkedIn Talent Solutions: business.linkedin.com/talent-solutions
- U.S. Department of Labor (DOL): www.dol.gov
- Occupational Safety and Health Administration (OSHA): www.osha.gov
- International Labour Organization (ILO): www.ilo.org
- Workday: www.workday.com
- SuccessFactors (SAP): www.successfactors.com
- LinkedIn Learning: www.linkedin.com/learning